Railways of the
Modern Age since 1963

Railways of the Modern Age since 1963

By O. S. Nock

*Illustrated by
Clifford and
Wendy Meadway*

MACMILLAN PUBLISHING CO., INC.
New York

Macmillan Publishing Co., Inc.
866 Third Avenue, New York, N.Y. 10022

Library of Congress Cataloging in Publication Data

Nock, Oswald Stevens.
  Railways of the modern age since 1963.

  (Railways of the world in color)
  Includes index.
  1. Railroads. 2. Locomotives. I. Title.
TF20.N63 1976   385'.09'046   75-28489
ISBN 0-02-589760-8

First American Edition 1976

Printed in Great Britain

Introduction

The 150th Anniversary of the opening of the Stockton and Darlington Railway, the first public railway in the world, which will be celebrated in September 1975, comes at a time when railways everywhere are entering upon a veritably new age. It promises to be an age no less critical, no less exciting than any of those covered in the seven previous volumes in this series. However unlike its immediate predecessor *The Transition from Steam*, the book ushers in a time of intense creative and expansive activity rather than the very anxious period of severe recession in traffic that followed the end of World War II, and the realisation by some facile optimists in high places that the elimination of steam traction did not mean an overnight reversal of the downward plunging of traffic receipts! The ten years now under review have witnessed a resurgence of confidence in railways as a means of transportation in the modern age, by the development of those disciplines and techniques in which what is now sometimes referred to as 'guided transport on land' is so ideally suited.

Development in different parts of the world has not been uniform. The immediately preceding volume in this series concluded by brief reference to the inauguration of the epoch-marking Shin-Kansen network in Japan. The present volume continues the story of its astonishing success and wide extensions. But such a development could have had not the slightest financial justification in the more lightly populated countries of the world, nor again without colossal national investment by the governments concerned. In the highly developed countries of Western Europe, railways have established themselves as the fastest means of inter-city travel. The large-scale construction of modern motorways will not be able to compete with projected rail links between major social, business, industrial and cultural centres. These, many of which are already under way, are designed for continuous running at 185 m.p.h. (*300 km/h*) and will, of course, make times between one city centre and another which no individual highway transport, or internal airline can equal.

This situation has already been achieved in Great Britain over the shorter distances between London and the major provincial cities, such as Liverpool, Manchester, Birmingham and Leeds, by trains at present not exceeding 100 m.p.h. (*160 km/h*) in maximum speed, but which are likely to be upgraded in the near future. Great Britain has a density of traffic on some main lines which is unequalled anywhere in the world. The London Midland main line out of Euston, for example, has 'flights' of six express trains every hour throughout the day. These leave the terminus from 40 minutes after the hour to 10 minutes past the next with an average interval between trains of only 6 minutes, and their running

5

speed is 100 m.p.h. (*160 km/h*). The alternate half-hour, between the XX10 and the XX40 departures from Euston is used for track maintenance and the occasional slower train. But the fact that one can successfully and punctually run a series of six 100 m.p.h. (*160 km/h*) trains at 6 minute intervals every hour is a testimony to the reliability of the signalling and safety appliances now standard on British Railways, as well as to the efficiency of the electric locomotives used.

In the advanced countries of the world speed and regularity of transit is as vital in freight as in passenger service, and in Great Britain again many notable projects have come to fruition in recent years. There are the 'liner' trains which carry containers on flat trucks running at speeds of up to 75 m.p.h. (*120 km/h*), and 'nominated' freight trains chartered by major industrial companies for conveyance of special products. The latter include the 'car body' trains run for the Ford Motor Company between Halebank (Merseyside) and Dagenham, and the 'merry-go-round' coal trains running exclusively between collieries and specific electric generating stations. That such traffic, which is the virtual equivalent of a 'belt-conveyor' between one industrial process and another, can be operated amid the intense and varied ordinary traffic of British Railways is a tribute to the flexibility and potentialities of railway transportation in general.

To see the 'belt-conveyor' philosophy developed to its highest extent yet, however, one must travel far overseas. There are the 50 m.p.h. (*80 km/h*) iron-ore trains carrying 10,000 tons at a time from Koolyanobbing, Western Australia, to Fremantle, or the even heavier loads of the Hamersley Railway in North-Western Australia. Or again the 4-a-day procession of 12,000-ton coal trains from the Crowsnest Pass in British Columbia, to Vancouver, on the Canadian Pacific Railway, *en route* for Japan. The working of these trains involves some of the most highly sophisticated techniques in locomotive operation that the world has yet seen, with radio-controlled helper locomotives positioned roughly midway in a lengthy train. On railways confined entirely to mineral movements the locomotives are remotely controlled, with no operator at all riding on them. In Labrador can be seen the nearest thing that has yet been produced to a completely automatic railway.

In this new age of railways the old-time glamour of steam has been replaced by the wonders of electronics, and what in some cases has been achieved by skilled model engineers in the past, in the way of automatic control, has been translated into actuality – with all the stringent safety principles that are essential in passenger-carrying added. But while the aura and romance of the railway is moving from the station platforms to 'back stage' locations, there are thrills in plenty to be glimpsed at the lineside as the French *Etendard* flashes by at 125 m.p.h. (*200 km/h*), or the electrically hauled *Royal Scot* storms the once dreaded Shap Incline at 90 m.p.h.

(145 km/h), where its steam predecessors would be hard pressed to sustain as much as 40 m.p.h. (65 km/h). The trains of the new age are dressed in gay colours, and plant is installed to keep even the freighters looking smart and clean. Those working immense mineral trains overseas go into some dusty places, and those running at 100 m.p.h. (160 km/h) or more collect more insects on their windscreen than any fast motorist on an *autobahn*. These must be kept clean, and the fine colours displayed at their best.

Yet for all the modernity the affection for steam not only lingers, but is becoming good business. Railways that strove to wipe it away now find that the occasional steam-hauled excursion produces better filled carriages than many of their regular trains. All over the world steam locomotives that would otherwise have been scrapped, or at best retained as static museum pieces are being restored to working order and used to haul special excursion trains. In the colour section of this book you will find a number of these celebrated locomotives. One of the latest recruits to the 'old Brigade' is a Dutch 4-cylinder 4–6–0, while one of the famous 'Royal Hudson' 4–6–4s of the Canadian Pacific is now running excursions from North Vancouver up the British Columbia Railway. The 150th Anniversary of the Stockton and Darlington Railway is being marked by an interest and affection for railways everywhere greater than ever before.

THE COLOUR PLATES

1. **British Railways:** the advanced passenger train.

2. **French National Railways (S.N.C.F.):** the 'T.G.V. 001' high-speed turbo train.

3. **Turkish State Railways (T.C.D.D.):** 2,400 horsepower diesel-electric locomotive.

4. **Jugoslav State Railways:** five-car diesel-electric train.

5. **Royal State Railway of Thailand:** diesel-electric locomotive.

6. **Iraqi State Railway:** French-built diesel-electric locomotive.

7. **Portuguese Railways:** British-built 2,700 horse-power diesel-electric locomotive.

8. **South African Railways:** diesel-electric loco-motive.

9. **Spanish National Railways (R.E.N.F.E.):** the 'Virgen del Rosario'.

10. **Danish State Railways:** diesel-electric express passenger locomotive.

11. **National Railway of Mexico:** Canadian-built diesel-electric locomotive.

12. **M-K-T 'Katy':** diesel-electric locomotive.

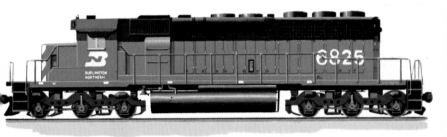

13. **Burlington Northern:** wide-body main line locomotive.

14. **Metropolitan and Long Island Railroad:** diesel railcar.

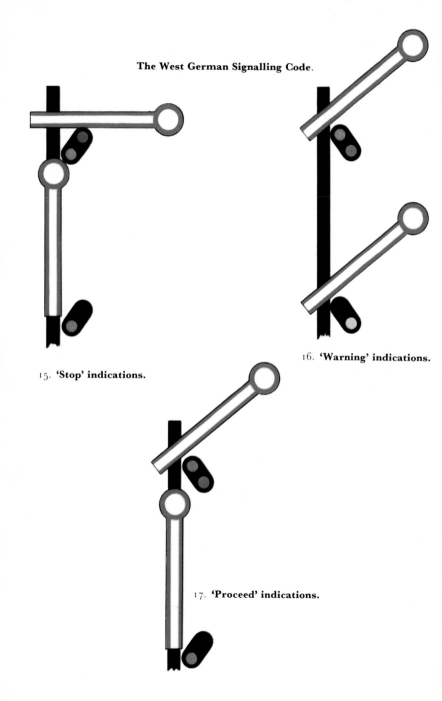

The West German Signalling Code.

15. **'Stop' indications.**

16. **'Warning' indications.**

17. **'Proceed' indications.**

The West German Signalling Code.

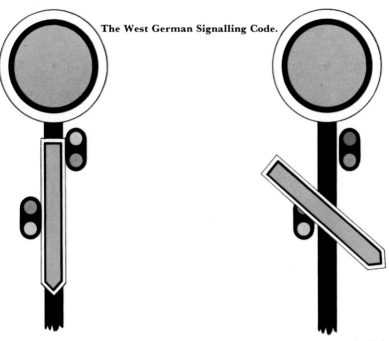

18. **Warning of 'stop' ahead.**

19. **Warning of 'caution' ahead.**

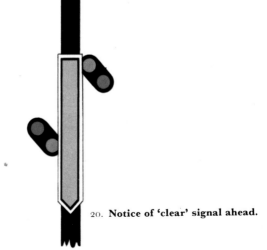

20. **Notice of 'clear' signal ahead.**

21. **Spanish National Railways (R.E.N.F.E.):** bi-current electric locomotive.

22. **Turkish State Railways (T.C.D.D.):** 25,000 volt dual-purpose electric locomotive.

23. **Belgian National Railways:** the quadricourant
express passenger locomotive.

24. **Swiss Federal Railways:** the 'Re 6/6' high-
power electric locomotive.

25. **Britain:** British Railways, Southern 'Merchant Navy' class 4–6–2 *Clan Line*.

26. **New Zealand:** the 'Ab' class 'Pacific' used for the 'Kingston Flyer'.

27. **Canadian Pacific Railway:** the 'Royal Hudson'
class 4–6–4 express locomotive.

28. **Netherlands State Railways:** 4-cylinder 4–6–0
express passenger locomotive.

29. Railways of the People's Republic of China:
4,600 horsepower diesel-electric locomotive.

30. Zambia Railways: 2,000 horsepower diesel-
electric locomotive.

31. **Jamaica Railway Corporation:** Canadian-built diesel-electric locomotive.

32. **Railways of the People's Republic of China:** French-built 4,000 horsepower diesel-electric locomotive.

33. **British Railways.**

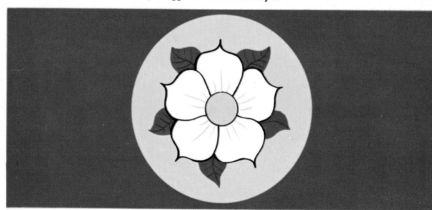

34. **British Columbia Railway.**

35. **Queensland Government Railways.**

36. **Illinois Central.**

37. **Burlington Northern.**

38. **Central Railway of Brazil.**

39. **British Railways:** high-capacity wagon for 'merry-go-round' coal trains.

40. **Great Britain, Blue Circle Group:** 100-ton cement wagon for use on British Railways.

41. **Coras Iompair Eireann:** container wagon.

42. **Central Railway of India:** 80-ton bogie covered wagon.

43. **Norwegian State Railways:** class 'E1 15' high-power electric locomotive for the ore traffic.

44. **Swedish State Railways:** The 'RC-2' high-speed express passenger locomotive.

45. **French National Railways (S.N.C.F.):** the epoch-marking 'BB-15001', electric express passenger locomotive.

46. **Portuguese Railways (C.P.):** 4,000 horsepower electric locomotive.

47. **British Railways:** rail fastening for high-speed
lines.

48. **The British pre-stressed reinforced concrete
sleeper.**

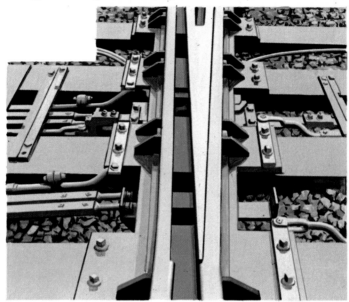

50. **Slab track:** worldwide introduction.

51. **Rhodesia Railways:** a 2–C–C–2 diesel-electric
locomotive, 'DE2' class.

52. **East African Railways:** a 2,000 horsepower
diesel-electric locomotive.

53. **Sudan Government Railways:** 1,500 horse-power diesel-electric locomotive.

54. **Nigerian Railways:** a Metro-Cammell-built diesel-electric Co+Co locomotive.

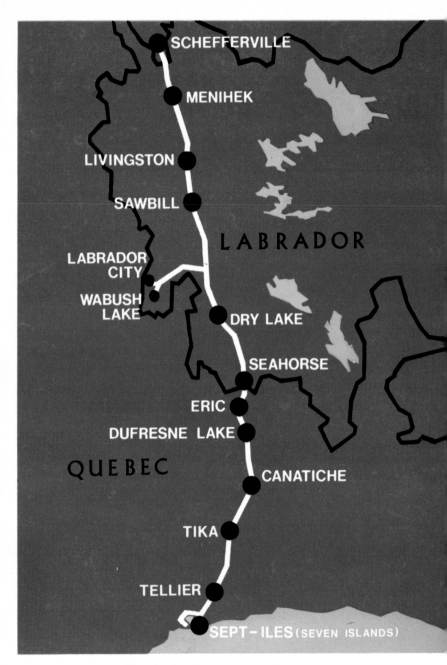

55. **The Quebec North Shore & Labrador:** a pictorial map.

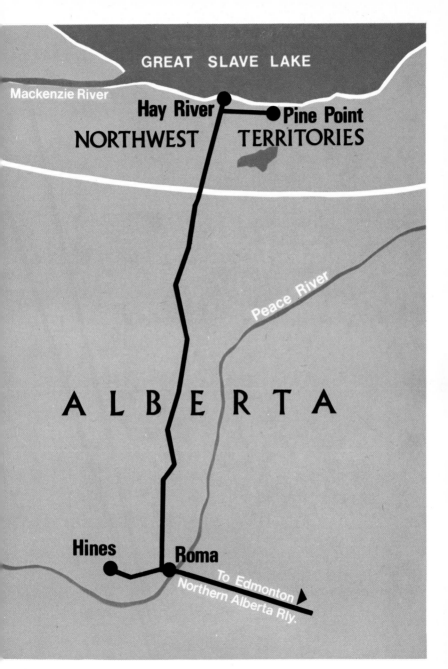

56. **The Great Slave Lake Railway, Northern Alberta.**

57. Quebec North Shore & Labrador Railway:
'GP-9' diesel-electric locomotive.

58. Driverless Electric Locomotive: Carol Lake
Railway.

59. **Canadian National Railways:** class 'MR 20a'
(diesel-electric) locomotive.

60. **Algoma Central Railway:** 3,000 horsepower
diesel-electric locomotive.

61. **U.S.S.R. State Railways:** dosage hopper wagon.

62. **Polish State Railways (P.K.P.):** self-discharging heavy mineral wagon.

63. **Italian State Railways:** Interfrigo refrigerator van.

64. **East German State Railways (D.R.):** a chemical container car.

65. **New Zealand Railways:** the 'Silver Fern' luxury railcar express.

66. **Swiss Federal Railways:** new four-car suburban electric express train set.

67. **Spanish National Railways (R.E.N.F.E.):** four-car diesel express train.

68. **Western Australian Government Railways:** the 'Prospector', fast diesel railcar train.

69. **French National Railways (S.N.C.F.):** 'Grand Confort' coach for T.E.E. trains.

70. **German Federal Railways:** dome-car of the 'Rheingold' express.

71. **German Federal Railways:** a 'D.S.G.' restaurant car.

72. **U.S.S.R. State Railways:** a modern main line passenger coach.

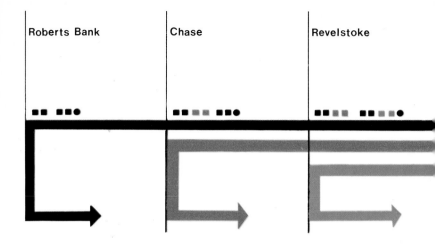

| Roberts Bank | Chase | Revelstoke |

73. **Canadian Pacific Railway:** pictorial diagram of the coal train route from the Crowsnest Pass.

74. **Canadian Pacific Railway:** 3,000 horsepower diesel-electric locomotive, as used on the Sparwood–Roberts Bank coal trains.

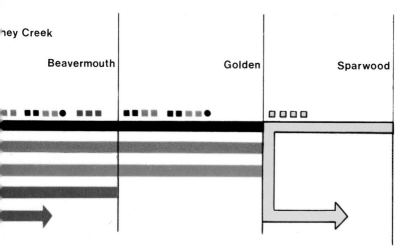

ney Creek

Beavermouth   Golden   Sparwood

75. **Canadian Pacific Railway:** One of the 'Robot'
units used in the coal train operation.

76. **Tunisia.**

77. **Japan.**

78. **Ghana.**

79. **The Netherlands.**

80. **Eire.**

81. **Finland.**

82. **Western Australian Government Railways:**
standard gauge 3,300 horsepower diesel-electric
locomotive, class 'L'.

83. **South Australia Railways:** 4 ft $8\frac{1}{2}$ in. $(1\cdot4\,m)$
gauge main line locomotive.

84. **British Railways:** the class '50' 2,700 horse-power high-speed locomotive.

85. **U.S.A.:** a 3,000 horsepower Co+Co diesel-electric for A.M.T.R.A.K.

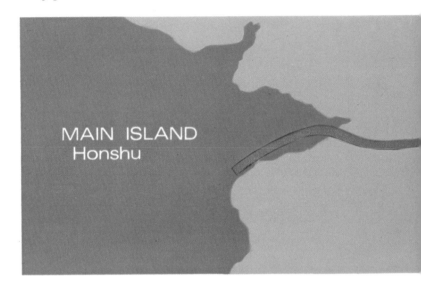

86. **Pictorial map showing route between islands of Honshu and Hokkaido.**

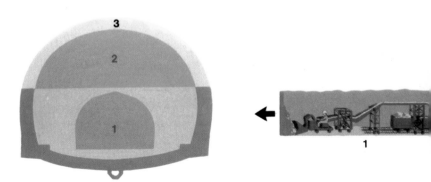

$\left.\begin{matrix} 87. \\ 88. \end{matrix}\right\}$ **Methods of excavation and construction.**

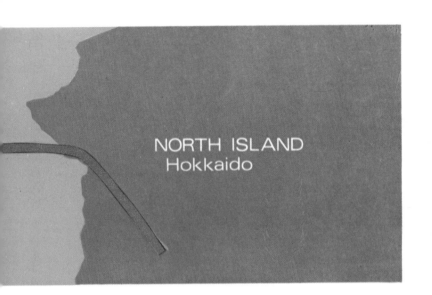

NORTH ISLAND
Hokkaido

2

3

89. **People's Republic of China:** 25,000 volt 50 cycle electric locomotive.

90. **Korean National Railroad:** Bo+Bo+Bo thyristor-controlled locomotive of 3,950 kW. capacity.

91. **Austrian Federal Railways:** general purpose electric locomotive, series 1042.500.

92. **Rumanian State Railways:** Swedish-built Co+ Co locomotive, 7,350 horsepower.

93. **Southern Railway, U.S.A.:** triple-deck 'auto rack' cars.

94. **Southern Pacific:** 'Vert-A-Pac' car carrier.

95. **Denver & Rio Grande Western:** 86 ft (*25 m*) high cube box-car.

96. **Louisville & Nashville:** the 'Stackback' flat car for truck haulage.

97. **Austrian Federal Railways:** the 'Transalpin'
fast multiple-unit train.

98. **British Railways:** the 'H.S.T.'

99. **Netherlands Railways:** high-speed inter-city electric train.

100. **The diesel 'T.E.E.' express train, 'Parsifal'.**

101. **S.N.C.F.:** the 'CC-6500' class 1,500-volt high-speed locomotive.

102. **German Federal Railways:** the '103' class high-speed locomotive.

103. **British Railways:** the class '87' electric locomotive.

104. **Jugoslav Railways:** Swedish-built type 'J2 441'
locomotive.

105. **Pakistan Western Railway:** British-built
electric main line locomotive.

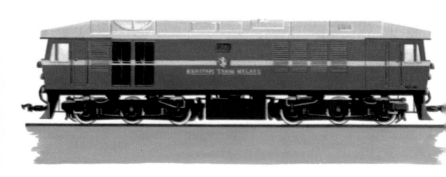

106. **Malayan Railways:** the '22' class Co+Co main
line diesel-electric locomotive.

107. **South Eastern Railway of India:** main line electric locomotive 'WAG3' class.

108. **Hungarian State Railways:** Bo+Bo general purpose electric locomotive.

109. **Wheel spacing change installation.**

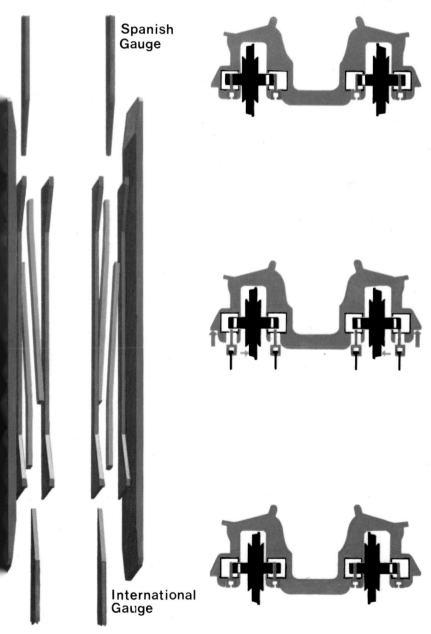

Spanish
Gauge

International
Gauge

110. **The stages of wheel change.**

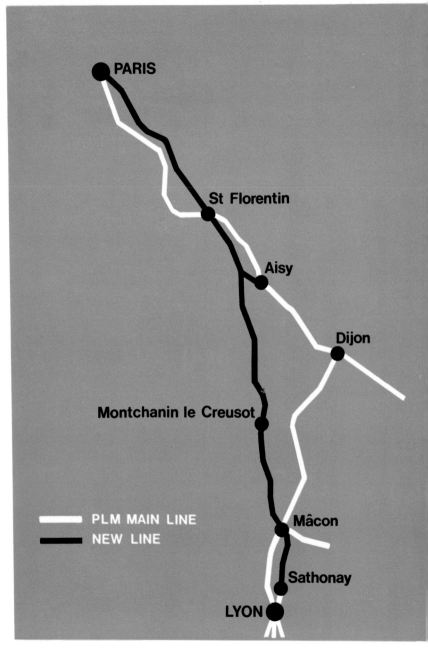

III. **Pictorial map of new Paris–Lyons high-speed line.**

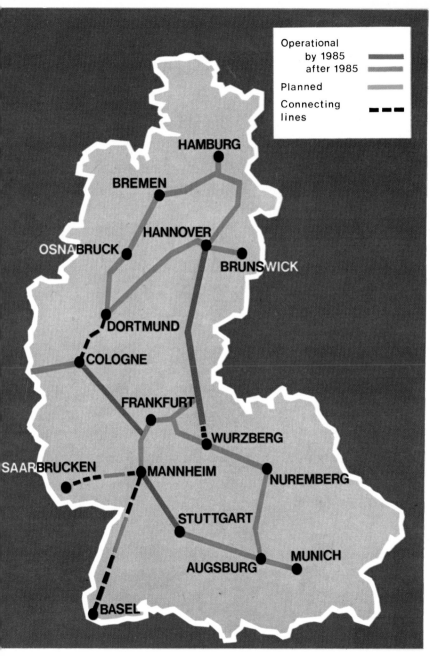

Operational
  by 1985
  after 1985
Planned
Connecting
lines

HAMBURG

BREMEN

HANNOVER

OSNABRUCK

BRUNSWICK

DORTMUND

COLOGNE

FRANKFURT

SAARBRUCKEN

WURZBERG

MANNHEIM

NUREMBERG

STUTTGART

MUNICH

AUGSBURG

BASEL

112. **Pictorial map showing new high-speed lines in West Germany.**

113. **Great Western Railway (England):** the preserved 4–6–0 locomotive *Burton Agnes Hall*.

114. **Canadian National Railways:** the preserved
'U–1–f' 4–8–2 locomotive No. 6060.

115. **South Australian Railways:** the preserved
lightweight 4–8–4 *Sir Malcolm Barclay-Harvey*.

116. **Cape Breton Steam Railway, Nova Scotia:**
the English 'Schools' class 4–4–0 *Repton*.

117. **Turkish Railways:** a Pullman seat passenger coach.

118. **Seaboard Coast Line:** one of the latest dining cars.

119. **British Railways:** the Mark III coach for high-speed trains.

120. **Spanish National Railways (R.E.N.F.E.):** coach of the Talgo train.

121. **South African Railways:** double-tier car-carrier.

122. **South Africa:** side dump wagon for Iscor.

123. **New Zealand Railways:** 42-ton bottom discharge coal hopper wagon.

124. **Victorian Railways:** bulk grain wagon.

125. **A Pennsylvania high-speed electric loco-motive, repainted in the A.M.T.R.A.K. colours.**

126. **The French-built turbo train.**

127. **The strikingly styled 'Metroliner'.**

128. **What the new super-power looks like.**

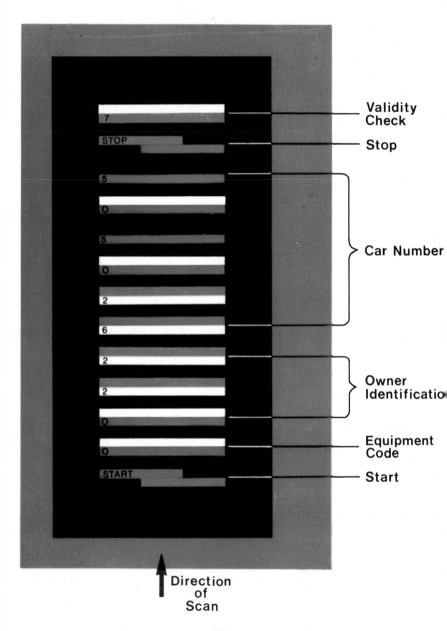

129. **Automatic car identification:** a colour coded panel, as seen on a Santa Fé car.

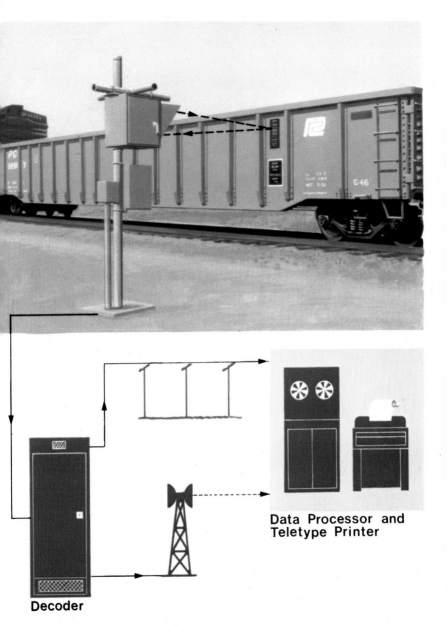

130. **Automatic car identification:** the detecting apparatus directed towards a Penn–Central car.

Decoder

Data Processor and Teletype Printer

132. **New South Wales Government Railways:** double-deck power car for Sydney suburban service.

133. **Rumanian State Railways:** double-decker train.

134. **New South Wales Government Railways:**
double-decker train for inter-urban service.

135. **C.P. Rail:** Montreal double-deck cars for the
Montreal suburban service.

136. **Union Pacific Railroad:** maximum power diesel-electric locomotive.

137. **Western Australian Government Railways:** 2,000 horsepower diesel-electric locomotive for 3 ft 6 in. (*1·2 m*) gauge lines.

138. **Erie–Lackawanna:** G.E.C. model 'U34 CH'
diesel-electric locomotive.

139. **Auto-Train Corporation:** G.E.C. 4,000 horsepower diesel-electric locomotive for car-carrier
trains.

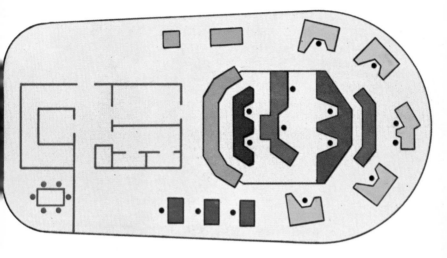

140. **West German Federal Railways:** diagram of
the signal control tower at Frankfurt.

141. **Frankfurt Signal Box:** inside the control room.

142. **West German Federal Railways (D.B.):** the
Frankfurt control tower.

143. **Queensland Government Railways:** the signal box at Rockhampton.

144. **British Railways:** the signal box at Preston, Lancs.

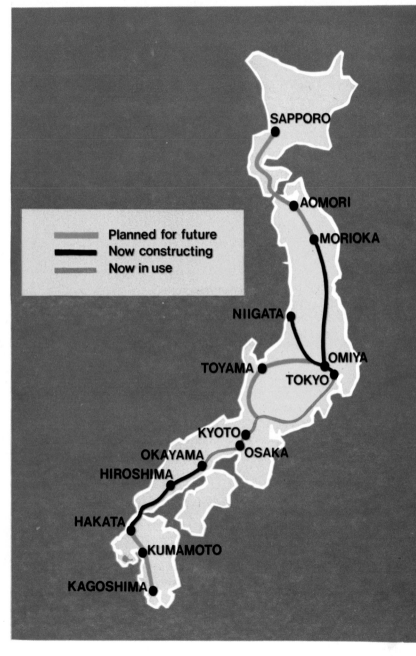

145. **Japanese National Railways:** pictorial map of nationwide Shin-Kansen network.

146. **Japanese National Railways:** a line-up of 'Hikari' lightning trains.

147. **Japanese National Railways:** the magnetic levitation research vehicle.

148. Black Mesa and Lake Powell Railroad:
50,000 volt fully automated electric locomotive.

149. Norwegian State Railways: Co–Co passenger
electric locomotive.

150. **Moroccan National Railways:** 2,750 kw electric locomotive.

151. **South Jersey Transit:** electric railcar for automatic train operation.

152. **East German State Railways:** the Warnemünde train ferry.

Railways of the
Modern Age Since 1963

1. **British Railways:** the advanced passenger train.

The whole trend of railway development in the advanced countries of the world at the present time is to accelerate passenger train services so as to provide a fully acceptable alternative for internal transport to the private motor car on the highways, and to the short-distance internal airlines. The electrification of the London Midland Region of British Railways, and the institution of a train service providing expresses at frequent regular intervals has been very successful in collecting the cream of the business traffic. Both London–Liverpool and London–Manchester take only a few minutes over the even 2½ hours without the need of scheduled speeds in excess of 100 m.p.h. (*160 km/h*). For longer distances however faster running is needed, and already the High Speed Diesel Train, H.S.T. (ref. 98), capable of regular running at 125 m.p.h. (*200 km/h*) is in revenue earning service. In this present age however, 125 m.p.h. (*200 km/h*) is not considered to be enough.

In the intricate and heavily utilised network of British Railways the problem would be to provide special tracks capable of taking higher speeds. While there is a definite need for considerably higher speed the likely clientele would not justify the construction of entirely new lines specially for the purpose, as has already been done with the Shin-Kansen lines in Japan (ref. 145–147). So the ingenuity of research engineers has been directed to the design of a train that can be run safely at speeds of at least 155 m.p.h. (*250 km/h*) on tracks normally carrying a maximum speed of 100 m.p.h. (*160 km/h*). Without going into the highly technical details of how it is done, the principle of the Advanced Passenger Train (A.P.T.) is that of causing the train to adjust itself to the curves by a tilting action of body in relation to the bogies, so that it can safely and comfortably negotiate existing curves at far higher speeds than are possible with conventional rolling stock. The train is still only in the experimental stage, but it is certainly a pointer towards the future.

2. **French National Railways (S.N.C.F.):** the 'TGV 001' high-speed turbo train.

The French Railways have the same kind of problem that exists in Great Britain, so far as the competition for inter-city traffic is concerned between the railway, the highways, and the air except that the distances between the major centres of population are greater. Development has so far centred upon a train capable of running continuously at 186 m.p.h. (*300 km/h*). Later in this book (ref. 111) the first route on which such a

89

train is likely to be introduced is discussed and illustrated. In the meantime an experimental train has been built, and tested at what is intended to be the normal running speed. The S.N.C.F. has in the former P.O.–Midi main line south of Bordeaux a route that is very favourable to the running of very high speeds, and it witnessed in 1955 some trial runs on which maximum speeds of more than 200 m.p.h. (*320 km/h*) were attained with standard electric locomotives.

The experimental train, consisting of one of the specially streamlined units at each end had three ordinary cars in between. These however are 'ordinary' only in the sense that they had no specially pointed features. The train is articulated throughout, so that the five units have a total of only six bogies. Also, like the already famous Japanese Shin-Kansen trains, every axle in the train is motored. Thus the length can be increased as necessary. The original experimental train provided accommodation for 300 passengers; to provide for 600 would require the same type of head and rear unit, and seven intermediate cars. The experimental train is powered by four gas turbines driving turbo-alternators which provide the electric current for driving the train. It was completed at the famous Alsthom works in Belfort, in March 1972, and made a number of trial runs on the well-aligned main line across the Plain of Alsace at speeds up to 150 m.p.h. (*220 km/h*). Then in July 1972 its trials were transferred to the line south of Bordeaux. These culminated

on 8 December 1972, by a run on which a maximum speed of 197 m.p.h. (*318 km/h*) was sustained for about 5 miles between Labouheyre and Facture. This type of train is intended to provide a service of 2 hours from Paris to Lyons – an *average* speed of 158 m.p.h. (*254 km/h*).

3–10. **Diesels in Worldwide Use.**

In this modern age the diesel locomotive has become just as much the basic form of traction on the railways of the world as the steam locomotive was in earlier days. In some countries, notably West Germany, the hydraulic system of transmission is favoured, but otherwise an overwhelming proportion of users have adopted the electric system. In this section of the book twelve interesting applications of diesel traction are illustrated. They range over four continents, and a variety of uses. It is this versatility that has won for the diesel its wide acceptance. Used singly, or in pairs for heavy loading it is used also for a high-speed express passenger train, as exemplified by the Danish No. 1401 (ref. 10) which is rated for a maximum speed of 90 m.p.h. (*145 km/h*). Reference is made later in this book (ref. 84) to the British class '50', which, used in pairs, were able to provide a greatly accelerated service to Scotland prior to electrification.

The diesel-electric locomotive is also ideal for very heavy work on severe gradients, at relatively low speeds. In comparison with steam locomotives that are of nominally the same capacity, the diesel-electric can exert a considerably greater tractive power at speeds below 20 m.p.h. (32 *km/h*), whereas the steam locomotive shows to greater advantage in the higher ranges of speed. It was for this reason that some of the earliest applications of diesel-electric traction in North America were on the extremely severe sections through the Rocky Mountains. There is also the invaluable feature of being able to couple diesels, like 'straight' electrics, in multiple. With steam traction if greater power than could be provided by one locomotive was needed, one had to resort to double heading, with not only an additional locomotive, but, of course, an additional crew. The facility of coupling diesels in multiple enables any number of locomotives to be controlled by a single driver, though in actual practice it is rare to see more than five at the leading end of any one train.

It might be questioned if the use of a large number of medium-powered locomotives is the most economical method of working. The diesel-electric, unlike the steam locomotive, is at its maximum efficiency when working at full power, and it has been found advantageous to have large fleets of medium-powered units, of 1,500 to 2,500 horsepower, which can be used singly, or coupled as necessary, to avoid having larger units of 3,000 horsepower or more, which on some of their duties would be run at considerably less than their maximum capacity. There are, of course, many applications today where larger locomotives are called for.

Another attribute of the diesel is illustrated by its use in countries such as Iraq, Mexico and South Africa, where there are lengthy sections crossing near-desert country, where water is scarce. The South African Railways provide a particularly interesting case. With ample supplies of good coal it has been the policy of that great administration to retain steam traction until such time as the lines concerned could be electrified. Steam has been retained in a number of major areas between the gradually expanding electrified areas centred upon the Reef, on the one hand, and Cape Town on the other. Then however there was the special case of South-West Africa. Traffic did not justify electrification, but the desert conditions made the operation of steam very difficult. It was there that the diesels have been very successfully introduced, and Figure 8 shows one of the most recent examples.

In Thailand (ref. 5) the first introduction of diesels was to some extent experimental. From the viewpoint of tractive power they were an attractive proposition for the hilly northern sections, but economic conditions precluded any large scale changeover from steam. As in South Africa an indigenous form of locomotive fuel was readily available in the local timber. The Royal State Railway purchased small batches of both diesel-electric (from the U.S.A.) and diesel-hydraulic (from West Germany) locomotives, and although no major replacement of steam is yet possible, it would seem that the diesel-electric system is likely to be the future standard.

91

Interesting and picturesquely styled examples of the modern diesel-electric are illustrated as representing latest practice in Spain and Portugal. The 'Virgen del Rosario' is referred to in more detail in connection with the train it hauls, the 'Talgo,' (ref. 120), but one of the most interesting European diesel trains of recent times is the five-car multiple-unit set, of which six have recently been built in France for the Zagreb Region of the Jugoslav State Railways (ref. 4). These are in every way *de luxe* trains, and have been designed for use in the popular tourist regions of the Dalmatian Coast, for a maximum speed of 74½ m.p.h. (*120 km/h*) and a sustained speed of 50 m.p.h. (*80 km/h*) up the 1 in 40 gradients that occur on these lines.

Unlike the ultra-high-speed trains (refs. 1 and 2) in Great Britain and France, these new Jugoslav trains are composed of vehicles each having two four-wheeled bogies. They are very long, measuring 82½ ft overall. The two motor coaches at each end seat 36 passengers, and the second and fourth cars, seat 54. The central car of the five-car train includes a bar, a train 'office', and accommodation for the train hostess, in addition to providing seating for 24 passengers taking light refreshments. The passenger accommodation is throughout of the open-saloon type, but of luxurious quality, while the buffet section is most attractively designed. There is a diesel engine in each of the motor coaches, providing power for six traction motors. The train itself is of lightweight construction,

and despite the great length of each of the cars, its total weight, unloaded, is no more than 220 tons.

11–13. The Diesel in North America.

The earliest practical applications of diesel traction on railways were in South America, with British-built equipment, but it was its introduction in North America that made the greatest impact upon railway traction policy all over the world. This phenomenon has been described and illustrated in the previous volume in this series, *Railways in the Transition from Steam*. Nevertheless the flood-tide of the diesel conquest of American railroading had scarcely begun to lose something of its peak momentum when there began, gradually at first, but then with increasing severity, a general recession in railway business. The rapid advance in the quality and extent of internal air services in the U.S.A. began to turn those most pressed for time away from the railways. No longer were the 'Twentieth Century Limited' and the 'Broadway Limited,' with their luxurious overnight service the premier means of travel between New York and Chicago; no longer was 'The Chief' the crack service between Chicago and Los Angeles. Businessmen travelled by air in a fraction of the time, and there came a sad day when the 'Twentieth Century Limited' ceased to run.

The effects of the recession snow-balled; staffs were reduced, the quality of personal service to the passenger was exorcised, and the standards of upkeep of trains and stations deteriorated. Less money was allocated for routine maintenance of track and equipment, and with each successive reduction came further fallings off in traffic. Freight took longer in transit; incidental damage to cargoes increased, and the companies engaged in long-distance trucking on the highways collected much of the business that shippers hesitated to put on to the railroads. The many railway systems in the U.S.A. were all privately owned, and the situation for most of them became critical. There were several cases of outright bankruptcy, and maintenance work on nearly all was cut to the very bone of safety in order to provide something with which to pay a meagre dividend to those whose money was invested in the individual companies. The fortunes of most of them sank to rock bottom.

Even so, out of a situation of seemingly unparalleled disaster in the history of railways has arisen a determination to survive, and to reclaim that position of eminence and universal esteem which the railways of the U.S.A. held no more than twenty-five years ago. Later in this book (refs. 125–8) the passenger developments under the auspices of A.M.T.R.A.K. are illustrated and described. Here reference is made to freight and local services. In this group of illustrations, however, is one that could be said to straddle the U.S.A. in that it depicts a locomotive built in Canada for service in Mexico. The Montreal Locomotive Works utilises A.L.C.O. designs, and the fine 3,000 horsepower diesel in

our picture is virtually identical to a design in widespread use in the U.S.A. and Canada, and which will be met with in many kinds of service, and many colours, in the course of this book. It is a larger version of many diesel-electric locomotives that have been built in Montreal for Mexico over the past twenty years.

While our picture (ref. 11) shows one of the latest A.L.C.O. designs as built by the Montreal Locomotive Company, the M-K-T unit (ref. 12) shows one of the newest 3,000 horsepower designs from the Electro-Motive Division of General Motors. The Missouri–Kansas–Texas Railroad, happily nicknamed the 'Katy', celebrated a hundred years of operation in 1970. It is a long and busy line, and is one of those American railways the name of which precisely describes its geographical extent. It has twin northern termini on the Missouri River, at Kansas City and at St. Louis. Main lines from these two converge at Parsons, which is a sextuple junction. In addition to the main line continuing south to the Gulf of Mexico, there is a subsidiary main line running south-west to Oklahoma City. The main line continues south through Dallas, the headquarters of the railway, to Granger, where it forks; the south-westerly arm goes to San Antonio where it makes connection with no fewer than six lines of the Southern Pacific, while the eastern arm runs through Houston to its terminus on the Gulf, at Galveston. The 'Katy' has 139 road-freight locomotives ranging in power from 1,500 horsepower, in the popular GP-7 'Geeps' of E.M.D. to the big 3,000 horsepower GP-40 which is illustrated.

In contrast to the units of the N. de M. and of the 'Katy', one of the latest diesels of the Burlington Northern (ref. 13) illustrates a new trend in what could be called the 'superficial' design. From the first introduction of the partially stream-lined nose-cab types from General Motors, diesel locomotive design, particularly for freight service, be-came more functional. For example they had outside walkways which provided ready access to the machinery through a continuous series of doors. This characteristic is to be seen in both the Katy and the Mexican units. In the new Burling-ton locomotives, put into service in 1971, the access platforms are once again closed in.

The Burlington Northern is an example of several amalgamations of American railroads. It was formed with the intention of reducing operating costs by the elimination of what were previously competitive services, and the closing down of redundant facilities. It involved the merger of three great transcon-tinental lines: the Great Northern which ran roughly parallel to the Canadian frontier, and was at one time a strong competitor of the Canadian Pacific, then there was the Northern Pacific, paralleling the Great Northern but about 50 to 100 miles (*80 to 160 kilometres*) south. These two lines provided parallel and competing lines from Duluth, Minneapolis and St Paul to Seattle and thence to Vancouver, in British

Columbia, and at the eastern end both connected into Chicago. The third constituent, the Chicago, Bur-lington and Quincy, ran due west from Chicago to Denver, while from Lincoln, Nebraska, another line ran north-westwards to join the Northern Pacific at Billings and provide a *third* route to the west coast. The Burlington route, in earlier days, was famed for its high-speed diesel-hauled 'Zephyr' trains.

14. Metropolitan and Long Island Railroad: diesel railcar.

While much has been made of the recession in traffic on the main lines of the U.S.A. commuter business has remained extremely heavy, if not necessarily profitable. Much has been done to improve services, and the quality of the rolling stock employed, and the electrical propel-led Budd railcars introduced in 1968 on the lines of the Metropolitan Transport Authority of New York City and of the Long Island Rail-road are excellent examples of taste-ful design and excellent performance. These cars, which run in 650 volt d.c. third rail territory – the same system of electrification as that of the Southern Region of British Railways – are designed for a maximum speed of 100 m.p.h. (*160 km/h*). They are arranged on the multiple unit principle, and can be made up into twelve-car trains. Such a train provides seating for no less than 1,440 passengers, with plenty of room for standing also! On straight level track a six-car train with a full seated load has the following ac-celerative capacity:

| Distance from standing start | | Time in | Average speed point-to-point | |
Miles	Kilometres	seconds	m.p.h.	km/h
1	1·60	70	51·4	82·66
2	3·21	115	80·0	128·74
4	6·43	195	90·0	144·83

A total of 620 of these cars have been put into service. Each axle is powered by a motor of 150 horsepower, and with no less than 600 horsepower the high performance is amply explained.

15–17. **The West German Signalling Code:** the 'stop' or home signal.

The code of signalling in West Germany is typical of that in use elsewhere in Europe where German influence was strong, and our illustration shows, alongside, the indications given by semaphore arms in the daytime, and the corresponding night indications by coloured lights. The same code has been adopted where day colour-light signals are used. It is a three-indication system. The uppermost semaphore horizontal indicates 'stop'; both arms inclined upwards indicates pass at caution, while the uppermost arm only inclined upwards is the all-clear signal. The corresponding light signal aspects are 'red'; 'green over yellow' and 'green'.

18–20. **The West German Signalling Code:** the 'warning', or 'distant' signal.

In semaphore territory the signalling code consists of a circular disc,

painted yellow, and a bar slightly longer than the semaphore arm of the stop signal. This assembly also provides three indications, in each case a warning of the aspect displayed by the stop signal ahead. These warning indications, by day, are highly distinctive. If the signal ahead is in the 'stop' position, the yellow disc of the warning signal is displayed and the yellow bar is vertical, in line with the signal mast. If the signal ahead is in the warning position, the 'distant' signal has the yellow disc displayed, but the bar is pivoted about its centre point, and is inclined diagonally downwards away from the track. The practice in Germany is to run on the right-hand track, as seen by the driver, and the signals are located to right of the running line. Advance notice of a clear signal ahead is given by display only of the yellow bar, vertically. The yellow disc is rotated about a horizontal axis, and being edge-on is practically invisible. The corresponding light signal aspects are, two yellows diagonally, in warning of a 'red'; a green and yellow, diagonally in warning of a caution; and two greens diagonally, as notice of a clear signal ahead.

21. **Spanish National Railways (R.E.N.F.E.):** bi-current electric locomotive.

One of the problems of railway electrification on the continent of Europe has been the different systems of traction adopted in the various countries, which at one time precluded anything in the way of international running. Spain, for example, had the additional complication of differences in rail gauge, although this has now been surmounted by the arrangements for gauge changing, illustrated under references 109 and 110 later in this book. But in Spain itself there are two different systems of electrification. All the earlier work, completed before the setting up of the national railway (R.E.N.F.E.), used the 1,500 volt d.c. system with overhead wire current collection, as originally favoured in France and Holland, and recommended as a future British standard as long ago as 1931. But after the formation of R.E.N.F.E. the position was reviewed, and a decision taken to adopt 3,000 volts d.c. as the future national standard. The fine locomotive illustrated, built in Spain but incorporating electrical equipment of Japanese design by the Mitsubishi organisation, is arranged to operate on either 1,500 or 3,000 volts d.c., as necessary. The controls are so interlocked that current cannot be taken from the overhead line unless the locomotive connections are correctly set for the appropriate electrical equipment.

22. Turkish State Railways (T.C.D.D.): 25,000 volt, dual-purpose electric locomotive.

At the time when some of the earliest systems of European railway electrification were installed, the administrations concerned had to arrange for their own power supplies, and huge generating plants like that of the Swiss Federal Railways at

Göschenen, utilising water power, were built. But the rapid extension of national electricity supply 'grids' in many countries has led not only to developments in railway power supply arrangements but also to reconsideration of the systems of traction. French trials of the high voltage of 25,000 a.c. at commercial frequency in the early 1950s were so successful that a decision was taken to adopt it as the future national standard, despite the already high commitment of many lines electrified at 1,500 volts d.c. A similar decision was taken in Great Britain, and in 1953-4 the Turkish State Railways adopted the same system for electrification of the suburban lines of Istanbul. The locomotive illustrated is one of a class built for main line working towards Ankara. They are equipped with a gear changing arrangement enabling them to be used in either express passenger or freight service. The locomotives were built in Western Europe by the '50 c/s Group', a consortium of four companies – two French, one German, and one Swiss, specialising in alternating current traction at the commercial frequency of 50 cycles per second.

23. Belgian National Railways: the quadricourant express passenger locomotive.

In the immediately preceding volume in this series *Railways in the Transition from Steam*, the remarkable quadricourant locomotives of the French National Railways were illustrated and described. The principles involved provide a striking illustration of the way in which modern electrical engineering science is overcoming the difficulties of the different forms of electrification existing in Europe. For in addition to the two systems in France, 1,500 volts d.c. and 25,000 volts a.c. there are the 3,000 volts d.c. of Belgium, Italy and the newer installations in Spain, and the 15,000 volts a.c. at $16\frac{2}{3}$ cycles per second standard in Germany, Austria and Switzerland. The French locomotives of the 'CC 40,000' class were designed to work on any of these systems, and had four pantographs. They are used on the through express trains between Paris and Brussels, some of which run non-stop, and all of which change from one system of traction to the other without stopping at the Franco–Belgian frontier. Hitherto these trains have all been worked by French locomotives and French crews; but the locomotive illustrated is one of a series recently introduced by the Belgian Railways and will enable them to participate in these workings and also to continue northwards into Holland if necessary, traversing 25,000 volt a.c., 3,000 volt d.c. and 1,500 volt d.c. lines in succession.

24. **Swiss Federal Railways:** the 'Re 6/6' high-power electric locomotive.

Despite the proven haulage capacity of the very fine 'Re 4/4' electric locomotives over the severe gradients of the Gotthard line, taking loads of 580 tons up the long adverse gradients at the maximum permitted speed of 47 m.p.h. (*75 km/h*), the loading of passenger trains is constantly on the increase, and the need has arisen to have locomotives capable of taking no less than 800 tons in passenger service. Hitherto, in instances of such heavy loading recourse has had to be made to double-heading. Because of the severe curvature of the route, and the increased length that seemed inevitable with more powerful locomotives, some experiments were made with an articulated frame and casing, in comparison to a conventional single non-articulated design. The locomotive itself was to be carried on three four-wheeled bogies. These tests showed that the conventional type would be satisfactory, and the very fine locomotive shown in our picture is the future standard for the heaviest work over this route. It operates on the standard Swiss system of traction, at 15,000 volts a.c. $16\frac{2}{3}$ cycles. The speed on the mountain gradients will be 50 m.p.h. (*80 km/h*), instead of the previous 47 m.p.h. (*75 km/h*), while on the straighter sections of line, in the approaches from Lucerne in the north, and from the Italian frontier, speeds up to 87 m.p.h. (*140 km/h*) are permitted.

25. **Preserved Steam Locomotives:** the British Railways, Southern Region, 'Merchant Navy' class 4–6–2 *Clan Line*.

The affection in which the steam locomotive is held is shown by the number of societies and groups formed, in many parts of the world, for not only preserving favourite engines, but for finding the means of keeping them in working order and for hauling special trains. This involves a vast amount of hard physical work on the part of the enthusiasts who undertake this, but also of astute and far-seeing management on the part of those who keep these endeavours solvent. Many of these ventures are quite private, and involve the purchase of condemned locomotives from scrapyards; but it is encouraging to find that in many parts of the world railway administrations are appreciating the publicity value and tourist attraction of well-organised steam excursions, and the following pages include interesting examples from New Zealand, Canada, and most recent of all, from Holland.

In Great Britain there are many locomotives preserved, and an increasing number are in full operable condition. A fine example is that illustrated, one of the 'Merchant Navy' class of 'Pacific' engines introduced in its original form by the Southern Railway in 1941. The chief mechanical engineer of that time, O. V. S. Bulleid, was planning for what he conceived as the post-war conditions of railway working, providing a locomotive of outstanding steaming capacity, on low-grade fuel, which, by having all the motion work fully enclosed in an oil bath would require a minimum of shed maintenance. Unfortunately the scheme did not work out quite as planned, and while the boiler was a great success, the engine portion had

to be rebuilt with conventional Walschaerts valve gear. At their best the original engines put up some fine performances; but their reliability was greatly increased by the rebuilding. The example now preserved in working order, the *Clan Line*, has the distinction of having achieved the highest speed fully authenticated by a Southern locomotive, 104 m.p.h. (*168 km/h*) near Axminster, Devon, while working the Atlantic Coast Express.

26. **New Zealand Railways:** the 'Ab' class 'Pacific' used for the 'Kingston Flyer'.

In December 1971 the New Zealand Railways inaugurated the daily working of a vintage steam train, because as the official statement expressed it: 'Steam locomotives served New Zealand faithfully for more than a century. . . .' Two 'Ab' class 'Pacific' locomotives were set aside for preservation for posterity, and this has made possible the re-introduction of the historic 'Kingston Flyer'. This train is not a flyer in the modern sense, because it takes 80 minutes to cover the 38 miles between Lumsden, in Southland, and Kingston, at the southern end of the beautiful Lake Wakatipu. But a set of period coaches has also been restored and in glorious scenery the ride itself is a delight, quite apart from the pleasure of the vintage locomotives and train. The 'Ab' Class was first introduced in 1915, and in all 152 were built. It is no exaggeration to say that they are some of the most successful locomotives on the 3 ft 6 in. (*1·05 m*) gauge ever to have worked south of the Equator. The two locomotives restored, and allocated to working the 'Kingston Flyer' are most gorgeously turned out with everything that can be polished simply glittering and the paintwork immaculate. It is, of course, entirely correct that they should be so, but those who remember them in their busiest working days, when for thirty years they were the mainstay of the New Zealand Railways motive power stud, will recall that there was rarely time to burnish them. It was enough that they were kept in first-rate mechanical condition.

27. **Canadian Pacific Railway:** the 'Royal Hudson' class 4–6–4 express locomotive.

The 'Royal Hudson' was one of the most famous classes of express passenger locomotive in North America. It was a development of the earlier class of C.P.R. 4–6–4, and received its famous name for the part engines of this class played in the working of the Royal Train, across Canada, when King George VI and Queen Elizabeth visited the Dominion in 1939. They were the standard type of express passenger locomotive on the transcontinental trains until the coming of the diesels, except on the very severe mountain section between Calgary and Revelstoke. An example of this class is in the museum of the Canadian Railway Historical Association at Delson, near Montreal, but No. 2860, the engine illustrated, was retained at Drake Street roundhouse, Vancouver, British Columbia, where the author had the pleasure of seeing her in 1971. Since then through the interest and enterprise of the British Columbia Railway, formerly the Pacific Great Eastern, engine No. 2860 has begun a new lease of life as a working unit. In striking out to the north from Vancouver the British Columbia Railway makes a winding and extremely picturesque way beside the waters of Howe Sound, with distant views of magnificent mountain ranges across the estuary, and from the summer of 1974 the company has been running steam-hauled excursions from North Vancouver, the southern passenger terminus of the line, to Squamish, at the head of the Sound, where the mechanical workshops of the B.C.R. are located. In the brilliant tuscan red livery of the C.P.R. and in such beautiful scenic surroundings, No. 2860 makes a brave sight.

28. **Netherlands State Railways:** 4-cylinder 4–6–0 express passenger locomotive.

The Dutch 4–6–0 locomotive No. 3737 had been a museum piece at Utrecht for many years, a fit representative of a numerous and justly famous engine design dating from 1910, and of which there were eventually 120 in service. The decision made in 1973 to restore No. 3737 to operable condition for running steam-hauled special trains was widely acclaimed in Holland. The class not only had a notable record of long, reliable service, but in another respect represented a milestone in the history of world locomotive practice. The railways of Holland were built and operated in conditions of peculiar difficulty. Much of the country is below sea level and protected against inundation only by the massive system of dykes. The ground is spongy, and not substantially weight-bearing, and in consequence the axle loading of locomotives had to be kept low. When it became necessary to have larger locomotives to haul the heavier trains of twentieth-century traffic, the mechanical engineering department was in some difficulty in producing a design that would meet requirements, without increasing the axle loading.

Close co-operation between the civil and mechanical engineering departments produced a solution of great importance for the future development of locomotive practice. It was ascertained that the existing express passenger locomotives of the 4–4–0 and 4–4–2 types, both having two cylinders inside the frames, developed a considerably increased loading on the track at speed due to the effect of the balance weights in the wheels. The weights were added to provide a balancing effect to the reciprocating parts, so that although the dead weight on the driving axles was no more than $14\frac{1}{2}$ tons, the effect of the 'hammer blow' due to the balance weights was such as to make the equivalent load at 60 m.p.h. (*96 km/h*) around 22 tons. If however a locomotive was built with *four* cylinders, all driving on the leading coupled axle, the machinery was completely balanced. There was no

hammer blow, and the civil engineer was prepared to accept an axle load of 16 tons. With this welcome concession the mechanical engineer was able to design a much more powerful locomotive, to haul train loads of more than 400 tons at 55 m.p.h. (*88 km/h*) on level track. The first thirty of the new engines were built by Beyer, Peacock & Co. of Manchester, but before this order was completed a further order had been placed with Werkspoor, of Amsterdam, and it is certainly appropriate that the engine preserved is the first of the class to be built in Holland. After the end of World War I further engines of the class were built by German firms, the last five, from Schwartzkopf of Berlin being delivered in 1928.

29. **Railways of the People's Republic of China:** 4,600 horsepower diesel-electric locomotive.

Following the proclamation of the People's Republic in October 1949, plans were drawn up for extensive modernisation of railways, and the integration of the several national and privately owned systems that had previously existed. The new government launched a great five-year plan for construction of new railways, and this was completed in 1957. In the following year a new one was launched that envisaged the construction of fifty-five new railways. In the electrification of certain busy routes the 25,000 volt a.c. system at 50 cycles per second was chosen, and later in this book one of the new French-built locomotives is illustrated. Elsewhere the modernisation has been with diesel traction, and our picture shows one of a batch of thirty very powerful diesel-electric locomotives of 4,600 horsepower built by Henschel, of Kassel, West Germany. The Chinese main lines include sections of very heavy grading, and the locomotive illustrated should be ideal for such duties.

30. **Zambia Railways:** 2,000 horsepower diesel-electric locomotive.

The Zambia Railways came into existence in July 1967. They consist of what were originally the lines in Northern Rhodesia, beginning at the crossing of the Victoria Falls, and forming part of what Cecil Rhodes conceived as the Cape to Cairo line. When Zambia (Northern Rhodesia) emerged as an independent country the rolling stock of the original Rhodesia Railways was divided in approximate proportions to the traffic obtaining. In particular the heavy mineral trains were hauled to and from the frontier point at the Victoria Falls by Beyer-Garratt locomotives of the Rhodesian 20th Class. More recently however the Zambia Railways have obtained a number of diesel-electric locomotives, and although painted in striking and distinctive colours the locomotive illustrated is actually one of the standard 2,000 horsepower models marketed by the General Electric Co. of America. The Zambia Railways are progressing towards a preponderance of diesels. Interchange of traffic over the Victoria

Falls bridge is now made by propelling the trains across from either side.

31. **Jamaica Railway Corporation:** Canadian-built diesel-electric locomotive.

This administration includes the oldest section of railway in the British colonial empire, the 14 mile stretch between the capital city of Kingston and Angels, which was open as early as 1845. Today that original line continues northward from Angels to the north coast of the island and then turns eastward along the coast to a terminus at Port Antonio. The longer main line diverges from the original route at Spanish Town, 4 miles short of Angels, and continues westward along the length of the island, finally turning north to reach a coastal terminus at Montego Bay. The total mileage now is about 205, laid entirely on the 4 ft $8\frac{1}{2}$ in. ($1\cdot4$ m) gauge. Most of the passenger services today are operated by diesel multiple-unit railcars, but for freight working the Corporation owns twenty main line locomotives, all diesel-electric; the system was in fact completely dieselised several years ago. Our picture shows one of the latest diesel-electric main line locomotives, built by M.L.W. Industries of Montreal. It is one of the standard range of A.L.C.O. designs that are marketed by M.L.W., there being variations identical in general appearance, but otherwise with six-wheeled, and four-wheeled bogies. The Jamaican example is one of the smaller variety of 1,500 horse-power.

32. Railways of the People's Republic of China: French-built 4,000 horsepower diesel-electric locomotive.

As a further example of the latest forms of motive power in China, this French product, one of fifteen built by Alsthom, makes an interesting contrast to the Henschel product (ref. 29). The design was to a large extent inspired by the S.N.C.F. '72,000' class of diesel-electrics of which ninety were built by Alsthom. The outward appearance is however quite different, for the '72,000' series have the distinctive front end styling that is characteristic of the latest S.N.C.F. locomotives whether electric or diesel, and which can be seen in the illustrations, references 101, 149 and 152 in this book. The Chinese locomotives are intended to work on very heavy gradients and in extremes of temperature and altitude. The temperature may vary between $\pm40°C$, that is $105°F$ and $-40°F$. while certain of the routes attain an altitude of more than 3,000 ft ($914\ m$) above sea level. At that altitude the capacity of the locomotive is reduced to about 3,700 horsepower, and in view of the heavy loads, arrangements have been made for two locomotives to be coupled in multiple. Before shipment from France the first few of these locomotives were tested on the original 25,000 volt a.c. line between Valenciennes and Thionville.

33–35. Crests and Symbols: British Commonwealth.

In the days of the old independent railway companies of the United Kingdom, much store and not a little prestige was set upon the insignia adopted by individual companies. Some of these indeed far exceeded the bounds of heraldic authority and had they been sought would almost certainly not have been granted! It was not until the Great Western Railway sought Royal permission to name a locomotive *King George V* that any heraldic scrutiny seems to have been made of the devices carried on the sides of railway locomotives and carriages, and then the only survivor among the major company insignia, that of the G.W.R., was pronounced heraldically unacceptable.

Today railways in many parts of the world have adopted symbols, or 'logos', to mark their identity. Some of these are ingenious in design, while are significant of the modern trend in carrying what could be termed a 'trade mark'. The British Railways' device signifies a double line railway, the arrows indicating running in the up and down directions. Today, however, when modern signalling and control methods are being applied, some double-line routes are being equipped for either direction running on each track. The floral device of the British Columbia Railway is rather apart from the rest, while that of Queensland is no more than a neat integration of the letters Q.R. in a modern image.

36–38. **Crests and Symbols:** the Americas.

The 'trade mark' of the Burlington Northern in its play with the letters B.N. is quite ingenious. It is known as the corporate signature upon which the company attaches great importance. It is regarded as having potential to project and enhance the identity of a corporation. It was all the more important in the case of the Burlington since it was an amalgamation of three large railroads and one smaller one, two of which, the Great Northern and the Northern Pacific, had very distinct 'trade marks' of their own prior to the amalgamation.

In South America the Central Railway of Brazil has adopted a 'double line junction' device, while the Illinois Central, one of the oldest railroads in the U.S.A. has again relied upon the clever juxtaposition of the initials. This line has now amalgamated with the Gulf, Mobile and Ohio, and is now the Illinois Central Gulf; but whether any change will be made in its corporate signature is not known at the moment.

39. **British Railways:** high-capacity wagon for 'merry-go-round' coal trains.

In former years the operation of coal trains was one of the most time-consuming and inefficient traffics in Great Britain. Coal was collected in small consignments from a great number of individual collieries, and conveyed in privately owned wagons to an equal diversity of destinations, much of it for local industrial and domestic use. But the great change in domestic heating and cooking practice, together with the setting up of smokeless zones in large towns has largely eliminated the individual load of coal, and substituted the running of black loads direct from the collieries to the central power stations. The 'merry-go-round' system of trains running in a continuous circuit was developed to convey coal from mines to power stations allowing the high-capacity wagons to be automatically unloaded while the train obviates the necessity of any marshalling, as the rake of wagons remains unchanged, and coupled to the locomotive throughout the loading processes.

40. **Great Britain, Blue Circle Group:** 100-ton cement wagon for use on British Railways.

While the private owner's wagon for individual loads has disappeared from British Railways, every encouragement has been given to the development of what are known as the 'nominated freight trains', chartered by large industrial concerns for conveyance of their products in block loads at regular scheduled times, often in their own wagons of specialised design. Of this new kind of traffic that for the Blue Circle Group, conveying cement in bulk, provides an interesting example. Our illustration shows one of the 100-ton bogie wagons built by

Metro-Cammell Ltd, which were developed from the success achieved with the 45-ton four-wheeled wagons introduced for this traffic in 1963. The new bogie vehicles, introduced in 1970, are of lightweight construction, and provide capacity for a payload of 78 tons, and are designed for running up to a maximum speed of 60 m.p.h. (*96 km/h*). They are equipped with the Westinghouse air brake, an automatic changeover valve which alters the braking force applied to the wheels according to whether the vehicle is empty or loaded.

41. **Coras Iompair Eireann:** container wagon.

In recent years the railways of the Irish Free State have been subjected to a severe progress of pruning and rationalisation. The picturesque narrow gauge lines have mostly disappeared, and the closure of branch lines on the 5 ft 3 in. (*1·6 m*) gauge has been carried out with a ruthlessness surpassing much of that experienced in Great Britain. But what has been left in Eire has been thoroughly modernised, and with diesel traction taking the place of steam, and contemporary practice in Great Britain, America, and the continent of Europe carefully studied, the present network is a closely knit entity. Colour light signalling is in process of installation on the Dublin and Cork main line, and the introduction of container trains is a further sign of the times. Our picture shows an exceptionally large container load.

42. **Central Railway of India:** 80-ton bogie covered wagon.

The long distances to be covered by the majority of through freight trains in India, and the extremes of climate experienced at different times of the year call for special designs of wagons to ensure the delivery of goods in prime condition. At one time most of the rolling stock for Indian railways was supplied by British manufacturers. But the old established firm of Burn & Co. in Howrah, West Bengal, has gradually been taking an increasing share of this business, and a large number of notable vehicles, some of highly specialised design, have been built in recent years. Our illustration shows a high-capacity bogie covered wagon, fitted with roller-bearing axleboxes. The British type of screw coupling is used, though an increasing number of Indian vehicles have centre-couplers while retaining the British type of buffing gear. These vehicles are fitted with the vacuum automatic brake which is standard throughout India. The principal constituent of the present Central Railway was the Great Indian Peninsula Railway.

43. **Norwegian State Railways:** class 'E1 15' high-power electric locomotive for the ore traffic.

In the far north of Norway, well within the Arctic Circle there is a short length of railway quite isolated from the rest of the State system. It leads to the Swedish frontier from the historic port of Narvik, and although only 20 miles (*32 km*) long is of immense importance for the great volume of iron-ore traffic passing. Just across the Swedish frontier is the station of Riksgränsen, and from there runs a continuous line to Stockholm. This line to Narvik is therefore more of an appendage to the Swedish railway system than the Norwegian, although it is worked by Norway, and it carries the huge total of 20 million tons of ore annually. It is in extremely mountainous country, and the six electric locomotives of the 'El 15' class, put into service in 1967, are very powerful. They operate on the 15,000 volt a.c. system at 16⅔ cycles per second, and with a one hour rating of 7,350 horsepower they have a starting tractive effort of 42 tons. Even this is not enough for the tremendous loads conveyed in one train, and it is usual to couple these huge locomotives in pairs, and provide a capacity of nearly 15,000 horsepower.

44. **Swedish State Railways:** the 'RC-2' high-speed express passenger locomotive.

Although the Swedish State Railways work in partnership with the Norwegian in operating the very heavy ore traffic to Narvik, and in other areas work many freight trains, in the south it is the passenger traffic which is important, and as in other parts of Europe there have been some striking accelerations of service in recent years. This is particularly the case between Stockholm and Gothenburg where the fastest train 'The Goteborgen', covers the 286 miles (*460 km*) between the two cities non-stop in 238

minutes, an average speed of 72 m.p.h. (*116 km/h*). Although time can be kept without greatly exceeding 80 m.p.h. the very fine 'RC-2' electric locomotives are permitted to run up to 100 m.p.h. (*160 km/h*) when necessary. They are relatively light, having an all-up weight of only 68½ tons, and yet capable of an output of 4,900 horse power on a one hour rating. The latter is no theoretical figure, for these locomotives are constantly performing very hard and fast work. That their very light weight does not render them liable to slipping, in bad rail conditions, is due to the thyristor control of their motors – explained in more detail in reference to the French locomotive (ref. 45).

45. **French National Railways (S.N.C.F.):** the epoch-marking 'BB-15001', electric express passenger locomotive.

In the development of electric locomotive practice modern techniques have enabled units of great power to be installed in vehicles of comparatively small overall weight, of which there is no more striking example than the British class '87', used on the London–Glasgow route. These locomotives have an overall weight of 80 tons, and yet they regularly develop about double the tractive power of the 160-ton steam locomotives previously in use on that route. They are at times susceptible to occasional slipping, on a bad rail. In the Scandinavian countries bad rail conditions are part of the normal 'way of life', and it is not without significance that thyristor control – one of the most effective means of combating slipping – has been notably developed by the Swedish firm of A.S.E.A. Instead of the conventional method of electric locomotive control, cutting out resistances step by step, the control is exercised by transistors in a continuous, and entirely smooth process. Additional refinements have been added to adjust, automatically, the control to each individual motor on the locomotive.

The latest development in French electric locomotive practice, as exemplified in the 'BB-15001', incorporates the thyristor control in a unit capable of an output of 6,200 horsepower, and a maximum permitted speed of 112 m.p.h. (*180 km/h*). But in this French locomotive, the prototype of which has now been followed by a production batch, a system of automatic control of the speed has been incorporated. If, for example, the maximum speed permitted on a certain section of line is 100 m.p.h. (*160 km/h*) the driver sets a pre-selecting lever to that figure, and the automatic control accelerates the train to 100 m.p.h. (*160 km/h*), and keeps it at that speed, whether running uphill or downhill. Such is the power of these locomotives that maximum line speed can be maintained on a gradient of 1 in 125 with a load of 600 tons; and if the gradient changes from 1 in 125 rising to 1 in 125 falling there is no change in the speed. The automatic control makes appropriate application of the rheostatic – or re-generative brake – to check the speed precisely downhill. At times as much as 700 amperes might be generated back into the overhead line. These remarkable locomotives are used on the Eastern Region main line of the S.N.C.F., between Paris and Strasbourg, which is electrified at 25,000 volts a.c. at 50 cycles per second. The later locomotives of this class are painted in the grey and crimson style, shown on the 'CC-6500' Class locomotive (ref. 101).

46. **Portuguese Railways (C.P.):** 4,000 horsepower electric express locomotive.

One can detect a strong 'family likeness' in outline between many of the latest products of the French locomotive building industry. It incorporates a design style that began with the quadricurrent electric locomotives used on the Paris–Brussels run, illustrated in the previous volume in this series, and can be seen in locomotives exported to China, Korea, and Belgium in addition to the one now under discussion. The Portuguese Railways are electrifying at 25,000 volts a.c. 50 cycles, and these new locomotives are very similar to the latest 'BB' types on the S.N.C.F., though of less tractive power. They are designed to haul passenger trains of 350 tons at 100 m.p.h. (*160 km/h*) and to haul freight trains of 800 tons up gradients of 1 in 72 at 25 m.p.h. (*40 km/h*). They have been designed for use on the main north-south line of the Portuguese Railways network between Lisbon and Oporto. The rail gauge is 5 ft 6 in. (*1.65 m*), as in Spain.

47. British Railways: rail fastening for high-speed lines.

The decision made by the British railway companies, some thirty years ago, to change from the time-honoured bull-head rail resting in a cast iron 'chair', and secured by an oaken key driven in brought with it a large number of incidental problems. The change in the shape of rail, to the flat-bottomed type was eminently sound, because it provided a greater lateral stiffness for the same weight of rail, and therefore gave promise of a track needing less in the way of day-to-day maintenance. At a time – just after the war – when experienced labour was scarce and costs were rising, this was a major consideration. Then, however, there came the question of securing the rails to the sleepers. In most overseas countries where flat-bottomed rails had been standard over a great number of years, the rails were laid flat on to the sleepers and spiked down directly, using a spike with a non-symmetrical head that overlapped the flange of the rail foot by about ¾ in. (*18 mm*). This was not considered good enough for British practice.

For a great number of years a cherished feature of British railway track had been the slight inclining of the rails inward, so as to provide a centering effect, and counteract any tendency on the part of locomotives or rolling stock to yaw, or nose from side to side when running. To retain this feature with flat-bottomed track necessitated the interposing of a specially shaped bed plate between the rail and the sleeper. This was accomplished simply enough, and although more expensive than most flat-bottomed track overseas, proved cheaper than the chair and key fastening previously standard in Great Britain. But then it was considered necessary to provide some security in fastening down greater than that of a simple spike. A degree of elasticity in the fastening was felt essential, and since the decision to adopt flat-bottomed rails was taken a number of designs have been produced, and given extended trial.

The form that has won the widest acceptance and is now being used as a standard is that produced by Pandrol Ltd., and the recipient of a United Kingdom Design Council Engineering Award for 1974. It has proved very successful in the heaviest service on the fastest and most intensively used main line in Great Britain, and before long nearly 100 million of these fastenings will have been supplied. The form of the spring with one end inserted in a socket resting against the flange of the rail ensures that the 'toe load' on the rail flange remains constant, regardless of temperature or weather conditions.

48. The British Pre-stressed Reinforced Concrete Sleeper.

A problem that would have faced the permanent way engineers of British Railways, whether flat-bottomed rails had been introduced or not, was the supply of sleepers. By the end of

World War II the days were in any case long past when ample supplies of Baltic pine were available at an economic rate, and in the difficult years between the two world wars many experiments had been made with steel sleepers, with the twofold object of finding an alternative to imported timber, the price of which had rocketed, and of assisting the British steel industry, which was then suffering acutely from the worldwide depression in trade. But steel sleepers did not prove a satisfactory alternative to timber, and war conditions soon produced an insatiable demand for steel for other purposes. Since then much development work has been carried out with concrete sleepers; and while one can never say that 'finality' has been reached in any feature of railway equipment – such is the pace of evolution today – the pre-stressed concrete type of sleeper has so far withstood the test of the most sustained service conditions to be found anywhere in the world. On the electrified London Midland line from Euston there are six expresses every hour all travelling at speeds up to 100 m.p.h. (*160 km/h*). The pre-stressed concrete sleeper was used when the line was prepared for the inauguration of this very heavy traffic in 1966. When the time came for its extension to Glasgow the experience with this sleeper had been such that it was adopted once again.

49. **The Swing-nose Crossing:** British Railways.

From the earliest days of railways the conventional type of points and crossings involved a gap to be spanned at the nose of the crossing. This was inherently a source of weakness, liable to give a jolt to the vehicle and lead to wear on the actual nose, and the point of rejoining the continuous rail. To minimise the wear of rails elaborate assemblies were cast, in high-resistance steel to embrace whole crossings, but these could not be conveniently applied to the simple 'nose' layout, in an ordinary turnout. It was to meet this difficulty that the 'swing-nose' crossing was introduced. In this arrangement the nose of the crossing is treated like a switch blade, and it is moved from one position to the other according to the setting of the points themselves. The operating mechanism is connected to the switch movement, and the swing nose is moved simultaneously, by a hydraulic mechanism.

50. **Slab Track:** worldwide introduction.

The problems of track maintenance under fast and heavy traffic are universal, and on railways in all countries means are being introduced for mechanising many of the routine operations. In the search for a form of track that 'stays put' to a greater extent than anything previously in use the wheel is tending to come full circle. In the earliest days of railways track was laid on large stone blocks set deeply into the ground, and numerous attempts were made to secure rigidity of mounting. With the rather primitive methods of vehicle suspension this rigidity led to much rough riding and breakage of springs, and what became the traditional form of track in all countries, laid on transverse sleepers embedded in various kinds of ballast was adopted instead. In recent years, however, with modern highly sophisticated methods of locomotive and coach suspension, opinion is turning once again to track laid upon reinforced concrete slabs. It is being used in the long tunnels and on the viaducts of the later extensions of the Shin-Kansen network in Japan; it is being introduced in Germany, while in France an experiment length is in service on the main line to Toulouse, as a trial for what was intended to be the track for the Channel Tunnel. In Great Britain an experimental length in the Midlands has been under observation for some time, and its first application on a main line has been made in the Eglinton Street tunnels, just outside Glasgow Central station, where the reduced height of such track provided a useful solution to what would have been a difficult problem – that of securing the additional headroom necessary for the overhead electric wires in a tunnel that would have been extremely expensive to enlarge.

51. **Rhodesia Railways:** a 2–C–C –2 diesel-electric locomotive, DE2 class.

The Rhodesia Railways are in process of a gradual changeover from steam to diesel traction, though the existence of the large Wankie coalfield on the north line from Bulawayo to the Victoria Falls, and the relative cheapness of the coal makes the changeover not so attractive as it might otherwise be. One of the problems of steam operation today is the increasing difficulty of obtaining spare parts – manufacturers such as Beyer, Peacock & Co. no longer being in the business. The policy in Rhodesia has been to change over to diesel operation those sections where water supplies are scarce, and retain steam on lines nearer to the Wankie coalfield. The approximate strength of the motive power stud now is about 80 diesels, 130 Beyer-Garratts of various types and power capacities, and about 100 ordinary steam tender engines. The diesels are used on the through passenger trains from Bulawayo to Salisbury, and thence to Umtali and Lourenço Marques. They have recently been introduced on the south line through Botswana to Mafeking. This used to be a particularly strenuous steam working with Garratt locomotives manned on the caboose system. Our picture shows one of the English Electric DE2 class, of 1,500 horsepower. More recently some powerful Canadian-built diesel electrics have been put to work, designated 'DE6'. These are used on the through trains to the Lourenço Marques line.

52. **East African Railways:** 2,000 horsepower diesel-electric locomotive.

The East African Railways, like the Rhodesia has been gradually changing over to diesel traction, and similarly the demarcation between the duties allocated to steam and diesel has been quite distinct. For some time now practically all passenger trains, on all sections, have been diesel worked, while diesels have performed most other duties from the capital city of Nairobi westwards to Nakuru. But the freights east of Nairobi are another matter. The line is entirely single-tracked, with long distances between passing loops, and to make the most of the line capacity the regularly scheduled freight trains are made up to very heavy tonnages. Even the latest diesels purchased from M.L.W. Industries, Montreal, could not cope with these loads singly, on the severe gradients of the route, and there are not enough diesels on the stud to permit their being used in pairs. The service requires the availability of twenty-seven locomotives continuously, and this duty is still performed by the enormous 59th class Beyer-Garratts of the 4–8–2 and 2–8–4 type illustrated in the previous volume of this series. The diesel shown in our picture is one of the 'M.L.W.' 2,000 horsepower class.

53. Sudan Government Railways: 1,500 horsepower diesel-electric locomotive.

The locomotive illustrated can be described as one of the 'first generation' of British diesel-electric exports. Technically it is of a standard engine design that was repeated in a great variety of locomotives exported all over the world, and developed from the basic English Electric type that was incorporated in the first main line diesels on a British railway, the prototype 10000 and 10001 of the London, Midland and Scottish in 1947. An external feature was the 'nose cab' which older locomotive engineers brought up in the steam tradition strongly favoured. This general design of locomotive achieved a high reputation for all-round reliability, in a great variety of operating conditions. This is high-lighted by the prevalence of desert lands traversed in the Sudan, although the British locomotive-building industry had had ample experience of working in that country through the supply of many steam locomotives including some large Beyer-Garratts.

54. Nigerian Railways: a Metro-Cammell-built Co + Co diesel-electric locomotive.

The present railway system dates from an amalgamation of two separate lines in 1912, of railways in the former distinct British colonial territories of Lagos and Southern Nigeria. The line in Lagos, from the capital city of that name, was the first to be opened, in 1901, to Ibadan, a distance of 80 miles. In Southern Nigeria the line ran inland from Port Harcourt, on the delta of the River Niger. These two lines have been gradually extended until to-day the system has a total route mileage of some 2,400, all on the 3 ft 6 in. gauge. Until recent years the motive power was entirely steam, but in conformity with the general trend of practice all over the world there has been a marked change to diesel traction, and the locomotive illustrated is a fine example of a British-built unit. The Co+Co wheel arrangement is used to distribute the weight over six axles and avoid excessive concentrated loading on the track.

55. The Quebec North Shore and Labrador Railway: a pictorial map.

One of the earliest of the 'new' railways of the world, the Q.N.S.&L. was projected to open up the immense iron-ore deposits in South Labrador which were becoming urgently necessary to supply the steel industries of the U.S.A. It was evident that the vast resources in Minnesota were being exhausted through the tremendous demands for steel in World War II, and further sources of supply had to be developed. The great deposits in Labrador, known for some time previously but not worked because of their remoteness, were surveyed anew, and plans were made for immediate development. These plans included the construction of a new railway to convey the ore from the mines in the neighbourhood of Carol Lake and Schefferville to Seven Islands for shipment up the St. Lawrence River, to the great steel producing centres of the U.S.A. The Quebec North Shore and Labrador Railway, with a main line 356 miles (573 km) long, was built as a first-class route, as indeed was vital seeing that its prime function was to convey 10 million tons of ore annually. It

also includes a very important branch from Ross Bay Junction, 224 miles (360 km) from Seven Islands to Labrador City, near to the enormous ore deposits of Carol Lake. But before this development began there was literally nothing in the area. Seven Islands was a small fishing village; Schefferville and Labrador City just did not exist. Even today there is no road in sight of the railway throughout its entire length. The only alternative to the trains are light aeroplanes. Through this wilderness a magnificently equipped railway has been built, with heavily ballasted track, good alignment, and remotely controlled colour-light signalling. Construction began in October 1950, and the northern terminus at Schefferville, then known as Knob Lake, was reached in February 1954. Construction continued through the intense Labrador winters, with most of the personnel and supplies flown in, to improvised landing fields along the route. Today the ore trains consist of three locomotives and 135 wagons conveying a payload of 11,000 tons and measuring exactly 1 mile (1·60 km) in length.

56. The Great Slave Lake Railway, Northern Alberta.

The Great Slave Lake lies north of the 60th Parallel of latitude, which in North-West Canada marks the boundary between the Province of Alberta and the North-West Territories. It lies in a remote and inhospitable region, but as a major catchment area for the Mackenzie

River was traditionally on one of the main lines of Arctic communication. After World War II there was some development in gold mining, but what led to the construction of this remarkable new railway was a sensational find of lead zinc ore at Pine Point, 55 miles (*88 km*) to the east of where the Hay River debouches into the Great Slave Lake. The 'find' was so important that the Government of Canada decided to build a standard gauge railway to link this potentially rich area with the railway system of Alberta. Between the Canadian National main line to the west, and the previous northernmost extent of railways in this region is the system of the Northern Alberta Railways, jointly owned by the Canadian National and the Canadian Pacific, and from Roma, on the N.A.R. the distance to Hay River is 377 miles (*606 km*) – a striking parallel to the line of the Quebec North Shore and Labrador northwards from Seven Islands. Construction of the Great Slave Lake Railway, which was entrusted to Canadian National, began in February 1962, and the line was opened throughout little more than three years later. The line is operated as a division of Canadian National, using General Motors, 1,700 horsepower diesel-electric locomotives. At the present time the traffic is in the development stage, with three loaded ore trains a week from Pine Point for the south; but other business is growing, and this new railway shows every sign of becoming one of the great industrial links in North-Western Canada.

57. Quebec North Shore and Labrador Railway: 'GP-9' diesel-electric locomotive.

At first one might think that the 'GP-9' locomotives, on this railway have little to distinguish them, except colour, from the many other groups of 'GP-9s' operating in Canada and the U.S.A.; but as may be gathered from the description of the railway itself under reference 55, the Q.N.S. &L. 'Geeps' have a very special function to perform. There are forty of them on the line, later reinforced by twenty-one of the 3,000 horsepower 'SD-40' type. In the course of a journey up the line by the thrice-weekly passenger trains we had passed no less than *seven* loaded ore trains in the 224 miles (*360 km*) between Seven Islands and Ross Bay Junction. Most of those were triple-headed, though some had a pair of the larger 'SD-40' locomotives. With such traffic it can well be appreciated that all locomotives are heavily utilised, and the maintenance, in the works at Seven Islands must be faultless. Some of the distances between passing loops are as much as 20 miles (*32 km*) apart, and a failure intermediately, and the consequent hold-up of this 'belt-conveyor' type of traffic could be very serious.

58. Driverless Electric Locomotive: Carol Lake Railway.

The Branch line from Ross Bay Junction on the Q.N.S.&L. leads to Labrador City, north of which is a large Mill and Crushing Plant of the Iron Ore Company of Canada. Some 6 miles (*10 km*) farther north lie the great iron ore deposits, which are nearly 40 per cent solid iron. The planned development here was to bring 80,000 tons (*81,280 tonnes*) of crude ore every day from the mountains to the crushing plant, and to do this was installed an entirely automatic railway. It was decided to work the ore from mine to crushing plant in nineteen-car trains, each car carrying 100 tons (*102 tonnes*), and with four such trains, each powered by an electric locomotive the necessary throughput could be maintained. Each of the four trains was required to make ten return trips a day, and the control of the electric locomotives is by the same principle of coded track circuits as on the Victoria Line tube railway in London. The Carol Lake line is single tracked throughout, and it is interesting when riding the driverless locomotives to see how the progress of each train is automatically regulated when two of them approach a crossing loop simultaneously from opposite directions!

59. **Canadian National Railways:** class 'MR 20a' diesel-electric locomotive.

The development of the diesel-electric locomotive is as continuous as that of steam in former years, and our picture of one of the latest types delivered from M.L.W. Industries, Montreal, shows some interesting features. Prominent among these is the modified type of cab, mounted in rear of a 'bonnet' that extends to the full width of the cab itself. The characteristic feature of the 'road-switcher' type of diesel-electric locomotive hitherto built both by General Motors and M.L.W. Industries, as exemplified by the Q.N.S.&L. type (ref. 57) was to have doors opening from the front of the cab on either side of the 'bonnet' leading on to the front platform; but in the latest design the front opening is through the bonnet itself. I have known the doors of the older type to become so packed up with snow and ice in wintry weather that the enginemen had to be dug out. These new Canadian National diesels of 2,000 horsepower, are used in the long transcontinental runs on heavy freight trains, usually working in multiple.

60. **Algoma Central Railway:** 3,000 horsepower diesel-electric locomotive.

The Algoma Central is primarily a freight carrier. Over the southern half of its 300 mile (*483 km*) long main line it operates three freight trains in each direction, and southbound, which is the heavier direction of loading the trains are generally made up to between 5,000 and 6,000 tons (*5,080 and 6,096 tonnes*). While none of the gradients are very long they are steep, with inclinations up to 1 in 60 and some begin very awkwardly from sharp curves and river crossings where severe speed restrictions are enforced. Exceptional tractive power is thus needed for maximum tonnage freight trains, and with 1,500 horsepower 'GP-7' diesels it is normal to use *five* of them in multiple. The introduction of the more powerful 'SD-40' class has enabled the heaviest trains to be operated by no more than three locomotives, having a combined horsepower of 9,000, against 7,500 for a *posse* of five 'GP-7s'. It has enabled the steepest grades to be climbed at higher speeds, and avoided the working of the diesel engines themselves at very low revolutions per minute. With the 'GP-7s' the speed of a maximum load train on the climb out of the Agawa Canyon to the summit level of the line south of Frater would often be no more than 10 m.p.h. (*16 km/h*).

61. U.S.S.R. State Railways: dosage hopper wagon.

The universal dosage hopper wagon, built by Konstal, of Chorzow, Poland, is designed for the purpose of transporting, and mechanically discharging track ballast in the construction and maintenance of railway lines. On a system having main lines the length of those of the Soviet Union, and running through territories that are for lengthy stretches but sparsely populated, any such aids to mechanised track maintenance are invaluable. The unloading is effected pneumatically, and depending upon requirements the ballast can be dumped on either, or both sides of the track, into the space between the rail, or over the full width of the formation. The mechanism is such that the dumping, and even spreading of the ballast is done simultaneously. The wagons are equipped with roller bearings,

continuous automatic air brakes on the Matrosov system, and automatic engaging centre couplers.

62. Polish State Railways (P.K.P.): self-discharging heavy mineral wagon.

Modern freight wagon design in all parts of the world reflects the urgent necessity of eliminating manual work in the loading and unloading of cargoes, and in Poland particularly the firm of Konstal has produced a remarkably diverse range of self-discharging wagons for various kinds of freight, and to the different requirements of many railway administrations. The large wagon illustrated is of a dual nature, in that the self-discharging feature can be applied separately to the two halves, if the belt or receptacle into which the load is being dumped were not large enough to take the entire consignment simultaneously. The action of self-discharging is effected by a de-enveloping movement, which opens bottom hoppers, and allows the contents to slide out sideways over a chute that carries the minerals, or other load clear of the wheels and the track rails.

63. Italian State Railways: Interfrigo refrigerator van.

The conveyance of frozen meat, fish, and indeed of all other edibles that the modern housewife keeps in a 'deep freeze' is organised on an international basis on the railways of Europe and today the four-wheeled long wheelbase covered vans of the Interfrigo organisation are familiar sights on many freight trains. The example illustrated is a particularly large vehicle attached, for servicing and maintenance purposes to the Italian State Railways. It is no less than 46 ft long – longer than many British bogie passenger carriages of sixty years ago, and has a maximum height of 14 ft ($4\cdot2$ m) above rail level. The long wheelbase, on a four-wheeled vehicle provides steady running, and permits such wagons to be included in freight trains running at the maximum speeds maintained in such traffic on the continent of Europe.

64. East German State Railways (D.R.): a chemical container car.

At one time the consist of a freight train, whether in Great Britain, Europe, or elsewhere, presented a dull assemblage of dun coloured four-wheeled wagons, covered vans, or in North America a lengthy string of box cars. Colour was almost completely absent, and so also was much variation in design. Today it is far otherwise. In the present book there are numerous examples of brightly painted vehicles, ones designed for single purpose utilisation. The elimination of steam traction and with it the accompanying dirt from coal burning exhausts has tempted many administrations to adopt gay and distinctive colours for special purpose cars so that they can be readily distinguished in classification yards, and, in certain cases, given the particular care in handling that their individual cargoes require. There can however be few more picturesque freight vehicles running today than

the chemical container car illustrated, built by the V.E.B. Waggonbau Niesky, in East Germany. The tank type containers, though ideal for transport of chemicals in bulk, represent a type of vehicle that is now becoming less exceptional in its shape in Europe. Very similar wagons, though not so gaily coloured, are in use in Hungary for the bulk transport of cement.

65. New Zealand Railways: the 'Silver Fern' luxury railcar express.

As on many railways in the world passenger traffic in New Zealand has declined greatly from its former levels, and with the superseding of steam traction a complete reorganisation of passenger train services has taken place. In the North Island, except in the case of the overnight service between Wellington and Auckland which is provided by a most luxurious sleeping car train, locomotive hauled, passenger traffic is catered for by fast railcars. These are mostly in two-car sets, which can be strengthened to four- or six-car formations at times of exceptional traffic. An interesting feature of this development is that certain services have the cars painted in distinctive colours – some red, some bright blue, and now the latest, the very elegant 'Silver Fern', illustrated, introduced at the end of 1972, and providing an all-daylight service between the two cities. There is seating for 96 passengers in what could be termed modern airline comfort, with hostess service, drinks and other light refreshments, and a luncheon stop for 20 minutes at Taihape. The southbound train leaves Auckland at 8 a.m. and the northbound leaves Wellington at 8.20 a.m. The journey time for the distance of 423 miles (*680 km*) is 11 hours. Except at Taihape the intermediate stops are of the briefest. The line passes through some fine scenery including the sight of an active volcano, from National Park station.

66. **Swiss Federal Railways:** new four-car suburban electric express train set.

While to many travellers the Swiss Federal Railways will be recalled primarily from the great Alpine routes, for the spiral locations leading to the great Gotthard and Lötschberg tunnels, and highly scenic runs like that alongside the Lake of Geneva, the principal cities – and particularly Zurich – have a substantial commuter traffic, and the smart new four-car sets have been designed to provide fast and comfortable travel in this business. Two coaches of the set are motored, taking current from overhead line at the standard Swiss pressure of 15,000 volts a.c., at $16\frac{2}{3}$ cycles per second. These trains have automatic electronic pre-set speed control equipment, whereby the driver sets the control to the maximum speed permitted over the line in question, and the electronic 'brain' accelerates the train to that speed as quickly as possible, and then maintains it there, irrespective of any changes in gradient on the line. The four-car sets are provided with automatic

couplers to make up longer trains to a maximum of twelve cars, if necessary. Each four-car set has seats for 224 second-class passengers, and 54 first-class, so that a twelve-car train full to capacity would be seating 1,118 people. The maximum service speed is 78 m.p.h. (*125 km*).

67. **Spanish National Railways (R.E.N.F.E.):** four-car diesel express train.

These very elegant new express train sets show the development of the 'airline' style of accommodation to a long-distance train but with the advantage of having the seats adjustable not only for inclination, but also for direction. Thus all the seats can be set so that the passengers are facing the direction of travel, or some may be reversed so that family parties of four, for example, may face each other. Individual coaches are very long, and with a highly developed system of suspension provide a very comfortable ride. The accommodation includes a cafeteria section and bar, and the train is of course air-conditioned throughout. While the exterior finish in gradations of steel-blue is inclined to be austere, the internal decor is light and gay. In the four-car sets only the leading and rearmost cars are motored; the second and third vehicles are trailers, and with the particular and handsome styling at the head and rear ends there is no suggestion at the moment that more than one four-car set would be used in a single train, by coupling in multiple.

68. Western Australian Government Railways: the 'Prospector', fast diesel railcar train.

Since the opening of the standard gauge line of the Western Australian Government Railways, between Kalgoorlie and Perth, the developments in train services have not been confined to the transcontinental 'Indian Pacific' through sleeping car trains, and the remarkable iron-ore runs from Koolyanobbing to Fremantle. The fast railcar services inaugurated between Perth and Kalgoorlie provide one of the fastest long-distance passenger trains in the whole of Australia. The 407 mile (655 km) run is made in approximately 8 hours. The power cars which seat 60 passengers, airline style, have two 375 horsepower diesel underfloor engines, while the trailer cars seat 64. Unlike their New Zealand counterparts the 'Prospector' trains provide a full meal service, again airline style. The route has been splendidly aligned, and on a journey I made we had plenty of fast running at over 60 m.p.h. (96 km/h). On one section indeed, from Northam to Cunderdin we covered this 35 mile (56 km) stretch in the level 35 minutes, start to stop, running at around 70 m.p.h. (112 km/h) for much of the distance intermediately.

69. French National Railways (S.N.C.F.): 'Grand Confort' coach for T.E.E. trains.

The development of very fast express train services in France with speeds maintained over lengthy sections of some routes at 125 m.p.h. (200 km/h) has necessitated as careful a development in rolling stock design as in provision of the locomotive power to attain and sustain such speeds. If the maintenance of such fast services had been accompanied by rough, or uncomfortable riding all the advantage of high speed would be nullified, particularly as the Trans-Europe Express network of which the French 125 m.p.h. (200 km/h) 'flyers' form a part, require the payment of a supplement, over and above the ordinary first-class fare. The 'Grand Confort' coaches introduced by the S.N.C.F. in 1969 are certainly magnificent vehicles. Some of these are of the open saloon type, known as 'A8tu', as shown in our picture, while others are of compartment type, 'A8u'. The seating accommodation in each is lavish, and in cars measuring more than 80 ft (24 m) over buffers and having a tare weight of 50 tons, there are seats for 46 in the 'A8tu' and 48 in the 'A8u'. Structurally they are built up to the maximum height permitted by the loading gauge, with the air conditioning apparatus in a space above the 'false ceiling', and they do indeed stand several inches above the height of the powerful locomotives that haul the trains.

70. German Federal Railways: dome-car of the 'Rheingold' express.

In West Germany one of the most famous of the T.E.E. trains is the 'Rheingold', running from Amsterdam to Geneva. It is one of those trains that collects through sections from various starting points, and distributes others towards the latter end of the journey. The 'Rheingold' has a section from the Hook of Holland, and that from Hannover includes the fine 'Vista-dome' car that is shown in our picture. This is a very attractive part of the train to travel in while the very scenic section beside the Rhine, between Cologne and Mainz is being traversed. It might be thought that because of the great height of the normal coaching stock on this luxurious train the view ahead from the vista-dome would be limited; but actually this is not so, and the provision of windows at the side down to seat level increases the general impression of an open air saloon. At this increased height above rail level one notices any slight rolling of the coach more than at normal seat level in a compartment; but on the really fast stretches south of Mainz, where the speed is around 100 m.p.h. (*160 km/h*) the going is usually very steady.

71. German Federal Railways: a 'D.S.G.' restaurant car.

In West Germany some restaurant car services are operated by the 'D.S.G.' company (Deutsche Speisewagen Gesellschaft) and when the striking looking cars illustrated were first introduced in 1962, for the 'Rheingold' service, they were finished in blue and cream and bore the initials 'D.S.G.' as illustrated. When they were incorporated in the T.E.E. group in 1965 the initials D.S.G. were suppressed, and the

cars subsequently painted in the cream and red standard for T.E.E. trains. Advantage has been taken of the great height of the Continental loading gauge to double-tier the kitchen part of the car. The three windows on a level with the inscription 'Speisewagen' are those of the kitchen 'office', while those immediately above, in the roof, are those of the kitchen itself. On this service the dining car, like the vista-dome car works through between Hannover and Geneva. The smart and efficient waitresses all speak several languages, and wear on their uniforms badges incorporating the flags of the countries whose languages they speak. When I last travelled on the 'Rheingold' the head waitress spoke five languages: English, French, German, Dutch and Italian!

72. U.S.S.R. State Railways: a modern main line passenger coach.

There is no lack of comfort in travelling on long-distance express trains in the Soviet Union today, and our picture shows an interesting example of a series built by the Polish firm of Cegielski. While these do not attain to the degree of extreme elegance represented by the French 'Grand Confort' stock they are nevertheless very fine, and provide a large amount of accommodation. The interior seating consists of two seats on each side of the centre gangway, and a total of 80 in the entire coach. These are reversible, if required, so that a family 'foursome' can be arranged to correspond with a window. The interior is cool and attractive, with upholstery and window curtains in greyish blue. The walls and ceiling are in a soft light brown, with a dark red-brown carpet. The general effect inside reminds one of the decor in the underground railway stations of Moscow, in its 'cool' style.

73. Canadian Pacific Railway: pictorial map of the coal train route from the Crowsnest Pass.

This is virtually another of the 'new' railways of Canada; for although the actual route involves practically no additional mileage the use to which it is being put is entirely new. In the late 1960s the need arose to export thousands of tons of coal daily from the East Kootenay area of British Columbia to Japan, and to move these tonnages from the Crowsnest Pass in the Rocky Mountains to a new deep-water port at Roberts Bank, 20 miles (*32 km*) south of Vancouver. This involved the setting up of an entirely new operational organisation, and some new techniques in application of the motive power. It was calculated that the required rate of export tonnage of coal could most efficiently be met by providing six new trains, which would shuttle backwards and forwards continuously over the 700 miles (*1,126 km*) between the loading loop at Sparwood mine site and Roberts Bank; originally a consist of 88 cars was envisaged, but this has subsequently been increased to 105. As each car carries a payload of 100 tons of coal, these trains were clearly going to provide a major problem in

haulage. Between Sparwood and Golden the gradients are not difficult, and to haul these trains of about 16,500 tons, four 3,000 horsepower diesels at the head end is adequate. The locomotives used over this first 223·7 miles (*359 km*) of the route couple off at Golden and return to Sparwood with a load of empties. After that, with the exceptional gradients of the Selkirk Range to surmount including the tremendous Beaver Hill with a maximum gradient of 1 in 45, special measures are needed, and the diagram beneath the map shows the locomotive movements adopted, when the service began with 88 car trains. The locomotives shown black on the diagram work through from Golden to Roberts Bank; those shown red go as far west as Chase, the green group go to Revelstoke, and those in blue are used only for assisting up the Beaver Hill. The locomotives proceed as far west as they are needed to provide power for the returning empties workings.

74. Canadian Pacific Railway: 3,000 horsepower diesel-electric locomotive, as used on the Sparwood–Roberts Bank coal trains.

A total of thirty-seven diesel-electric locomotives, each of 3,000 horsepower are required to operate the coal train movement, and normally four of these are on stand-by duty to allow for regular maintenance and repair work. From the diagram below the map it will be seen that no fewer than *eleven* locomotives are required to work a loaded train of

88 cars up the Beaver Hill. There are four at the leading end under the direct control of the driver; then there are four more, radio-controlled from the leading end somewhere near the middle of the train, and finally three more acting as a pusher unit, under a separate engineman near the rear of the train. This engineman is in radio communication with the man at the head-end. Since the increase in the maximum load from 88 to 105 cars, the number of locomotives on the Beaver Hill has been increased to *thirteen*: five radio-controlled units in the middle of the train, and a pusher unit of four near the rear end.

75. **Canadian Pacific Railway:** one of the 'Robot' units used in the coal train operation.

The 'Robot' unit is, in popular parlance, a gigantic 'black box', or 'electronic brain': an unmanned relay unit linking the lead and remote locomotives by radio control. The positioning of the robot and its slave locomotives is extremely important, because of the large number of curves in the line; and it is necessary to distribute the pull on the drawbars throughout the train so that there is no tendency to bunch the cars so that they are thrust outwards to derail on a curve. After much experimenting the formation was determined thus: 4 lead locomotives; 39 cars; 4 remote controlled slave locomotives; the robot unit; 34 cars; the 3-unit pusher; 15 cars; and the caboose, manned by a train conductor on radio voice communi-

cation with the lead and pusher enginemen.

76–78. **Crests and Symbols:** Asian and African railways.

The modern diesel and electric locomotives have a certain advantage over steam in that the gay colours in which they are so often bedecked lend themselves to additional forms of decoration. It is true that in the more spacious days of the pre-grouping companies in the United Kingdom, when drivers had their own engines, and the turns of duty were not unduly long, individual forms of decoration were added to smokebox doors, and sometimes to regulator handles; but in general smokebox doors – otherwise an advertising ground *par excellence* – went unadorned. Today the crescent and star of the Tunisian Railways is carried with pleasing effect on the front of diesel locomotives and railcars.

On the other hand, the Japanese National Railways, in devising a breathless, speed conscious rendering of the initials J.N.R. have, somewhat significantly, displayed it on the side of their remarkable 'magnetic levitation' car (ref. 147) which is to travel at 300 m.p.h. (*483 km/h*). The existing Japanese high-speed trains, like those of other countries, with which the speed is more than 100 m.p.h. (*160 km/h*) collect vast quantities of flies and other insects on their fronts, so that a 'corporate signature' could well be obliterated by journey's end, if it were displayed on the front. The third of this group, the very attractive device of the Ghana Railways, is displayed twice on each side of the latest diesel locomotives. With 'double-ended' non-steam locomotives it is sometimes the practice to display the number only at one end, as on British Railways; but Ghana puts the numbers at both ends and the insignia below it in each case.

79–81. **Crests and Symbols:** European railways.

The Netherlands State Railways have always been admirers of British practice, and in earlier years purchased many locomotives from British firms. They were much impressed by the 'corporate signature' device shown under reference 33, and their cartographers succeeded in producing the clever variation shown under reference 79, in which the double-line and two directional idea are neatly combined. The Irish railways, in pre-grouping days had some of the most artistic, and fanciful insignia of any in the British Isles, some of which have been portrayed in early volumes in this series. The new corporate signature of C.I.E. is however in keeping with modern trends. The last of this group might cause a certain amount of doubt from the initials displayed, because V.R. could be equally associated with the Victorian Railways in Australia, which administration uses the initials freely in its publicity. In this instance however they relate to the Finnish State Railways, the name of which, in the national language is 'Valtionrautatiet'.

82. **Western Australian Government Railways:** standard gauge 3,300 horsepower diesel-electric locomotive, class 'L'.

The standard gauge line of the W.A.G.R. from Kalgoorlie into Perth carries a heavy traffic. Iron-ore from Koolyanobbing to the Kwinana refinery, near Fremantle, is conveyed in trains each of ninety-six special bogie wagons, representing a gross trailing load of 9,000 tons (*9,144 tonnes*). While the final stretch of the westward run is gently downhill, on a magnificently graded track engineered with stupendous earthworks through the mountainous country of the Darling Range, much of the journey is over fairly level country in the wheat lands, and to maintain the schedules laid down ample locomotive power is needed. The standard ore trains have three of 'L' class diesels, a total engine horsepower of 9,900. They are also used on the 'Indian Pacific' but no more than a single locomotive is needed on this fast passenger train. At express speed I found them exceptionally smooth riding, though the excellence of the track on the standard gauge sections of the W.A.G.R. no doubt contribute to this pleasant travelling.

83. **South Australia Railways:** 4 ft 8½ in. (*1·4 m*) gauge main line locomotive.

South Australia is one of the states of the Commonwealth that contains three separate rail gauges. The station at Port Pirie was one of the places where trains on 5 ft 3 in.

($1\cdot6$ m), 4 ft 8½ in. ($1\cdot4$ m), and 3 ft 6 in. ($1\cdot2$ m) gauges could be seen alongside. But when Port Pirie was a curiosity the 4 ft 8½ in. ($1\cdot4$ m) gauge was that of the Commonwealth connecting line from the famous Trans-Australian railway across the Nullabor Plain. When the 'Indian Pacific' project took shape the former 3 ft 6 in. ($1\cdot2$ m) gauge line of the South Australian Railways leading up to the New South Wales border, and across it for a short distance to Broken Hill, had to be converted to 4 ft 8½ in. ($1\cdot4$ m), and so that the South Australian Railways could take their full share in the running of this splendid ocean to ocean through service, some new diesel electric locomotives had to be purchased. Hitherto all S.A.R. motive power had been either 5 ft 3 in. ($1\cdot6$ m) or 3 ft 6 in. ($1\cdot2$ m) gauge. The standard gauge trains working into Port Pirie were hauled by Commonwealth Railways locomotives. The new locomotives are of 3,000 horsepower, distinguished by having the striking insignia of the S.A.R. below their front windows.

84. **British Railways:** the class '50' 2,700 horsepower high-speed locomotive.

It was in 1962 that the English Electric Company built a new prototype diesel electric locomotive of 2,700 horsepower, and designated 'DP2'. It was given very extensive trials on British Railways as a result of which an order for fifty was placed with the company, for particular use on the West Coast main line between Crewe and Glasgow. Substantial accelerations of service were planned to bring the northern part of this famous route more into line with the standards being developed with electric traction south of Crewe. The first of the new locomotives, then numbered D400, went into service in 1967, and soon established a reputation for high speed and excellent performance. The class, now designated '50' were the first British diesel-electric locomotives to have automatic control of tractive effort, and to have a maximum service speed of 105 m.p.h. (170 km/h). To maintain the very fast schedules instituted in 1970, which required sustained speeds of around 70 m.p.h. (112 km/h) on rising gradients of 1 in 125, these locomotives were operated in pairs on express trains of 430 tons ($436\cdot6$ tonnes). Since the electrification of the line to Glasgow most of these locomotives have been transferred to the Western Region of British Railways.

85. **U.S.A.:** 3,000 horsepower Co+ Co diesel electric for A.M.T.R.A.K.

In 1970 an Act of Congress set up the National Railroad Passenger Corporation (A.M.T.R.A.K.) which is a public corporation with authority to support the operation of inter-city passenger trains in the United States with Federal funds. By that time the majority of the Class I railroads in the U.S.A. were in very serious financial circumstances, and the Act of Congress was passed to avoid the risk of a general collapse. By drastic rationalisation, and elimination of competitive routes a limited number of main lines were selected for A.M.T.R.A.K. passenger services to operate, such as no more than one through route from New York to Chicago; only one route each from Chicago to Los Angeles, to San Francisco and to Seattle, and so on. With the aid of Federal funds a vigorous attempt is being made to create a strong image for the A.M.T.R.A.K. organisation, with locomotives and rolling stock painted a striking new colour. Our picture shows one of the standard 3,000 horsepower diesel-electric locomotives in the new style.

86. The Japanese 'Channel Tunnel'.

The great success of the New Tokaido Line forming the pioneer section of the Shin-Kansen network of high speed railways has led to a national plan for an extension of the super-speed railways from the main island of Honshu to the large southern island of Kyushu, and to the mountainous northern island of Hokkaido. The railway connection planned is in each case by tunnel; but while the island of Kyushu is separated from Honshu by a narrow strait, the northern connection is much longer, and involves an undersea tunnel of much the same length as that proposed beneath the English Channel linking England and France. The pictorial map shows the route that will be taken, and on which construction is now well advanced. It has not been decided whether the railway through the

tunnel will consist of one 4 ft 8½ in. ($1 \cdot 4$ m) gauge line (that of the high-speed Shin-Kansen network) and one 3 ft 6 in. ($1 \cdot 2$ m) gauge line, which is that of the ordinary railways of Japan, or whether there should be two 'mixed gauge' lines. Surveys of traffic potential were being made when I was in Japan to determine what would be the most efficient arrangement.

87–88. The Honshu–Hokkaido Tunnel: Methods of excavation and construction.

The cross-sectional diagram shows the shape the tunnel will eventually have, with numbers indicating the order in which the excavations will be made. Part I is the pilot tunnel, in which is laid a rail-way to carry wagons for removing the spoil. As soon as the pilot tunnel is sufficiently advanced, and no underground hazards have been struck the main excavation is begun, in Part 2, and as the longitudinal sketch shows the spoil from this is loaded into wagons at Part I level. The next stages involve putting in the main arch, 3, and this involves the introduction of a concreting plant to install the lining of the arch. Once the excavation 2 is complete, and the arch 3 consolidated the remaining portions can be excavated, in the order shown in the cross-sectional diagram.

89. People's Republic of China: 25,000 volt, 50 cycle, electric locomotive.

This striking product of the 50 c/s Group is yet another example of the way in which the 25,000 volt, 50 cycles per second system of alternating current electrification is being adopted in many parts of the world. The Chinese decision to equip a very difficult mountain section in this way was taken in 1960, and the powerful locomotive illustrated is one of a class of forty ordered in 1970 from the 50 c/s Group in Europe, to which all members of the group supplied various parts. The electrical design is basically French, and based on the very successful experience in France itself with this system of traction. It is notable that the direct current traction motors are fed by thyristors, instead of the conventional method of using resistances on the rotary drum of a master controller. This more modern method produces a much smoother and efficient control of the acceleration, and has been used to most remarkable effect on some new electric locomotives in France itself (ref. 149). These powerful Chinese locomotives are equipped for regenerative braking, producing the major part of the braking effect by generating current and returning it to the overhead line, instead of needing heavy mechanical pressure between brake blocks and the wheels.

90. Korean National Railroad:
Bo+Bo+Bo thyristor-controlled locomotive of 3,950 k.w. capacity.

In its front end styling this further product of the European based 50 c/s Group is very similar to that of the latest electric locomotives on the S.N.C.F., but in all other respects it

is quite distinct. These Korean locomotives, which make up a class of sixty-six, are essentially heavy freight haulers, and have a maximum speed of no more than 52 m.p.h. (*83 km/h*). All six axles are powered, but instead of having two six-wheeled bogies, as in the largest French designs, there are three four-wheeled bogies. These locomotives formed part of the equipment of three main lines in the north of Korea, with a total route mileage of about 240 (*386 km*). It is interesting that although the line voltage is 25,000 a.c., the frequency is 60 cycles per second, instead of 50. This difference has no technical significance other than that of local conditions. The continuous rating of 3,950 kilowatts is equivalent to approximately 5,100 horsepower.

91. Austrian Federal Railways:
general purpose electric locomotive of series 1042.500.

The Austrian Federal Railway system includes a diversity of conditions for which to provide motive power. It is now almost entirely electric, using the 15,000 volt a.c. system at $16\frac{2}{3}$ cycles per second, as in Germany and Switzerland. There are heavy gradients to be surmounted, on the Arlberg route, and on the line to the south from Vienna, through the Semmering Pass, and the same locomotives have to operate at fairly high speed, particularly over the main line between Salzburg and Vienna. The locomotives have therefore been of a 'general purpose' type. The heaviest passenger workings are usually entrusted to large units of the Co + Co type, but the administration operates a large number of smaller locomotives of the Bo + Bo wheel arrangement, of which the 1042.500 series is one of the latest. Until recently the standard livery for Austrian electric locomotives was a dark green; but as with many other administrations, a gayer style has recently been adopted. These locomotives have a rated horsepower of about 2,500.

92. **Rumanian State Railways:** Swedish-built Co + Co locomotive, 7,350 horsepower.

This remarkable locomotive is yet another example of the use of the 25,000 volt a.c. traction system, at 50 c/s, and is a very powerful mixed-traffic unit. The normal maximum speed is 75 m.p.h. (*120 km/h*) but when not coupled in multiple, and on favourable stretches of line, a speed up to 100 m.p.h. (*160 km/h*) is permitted. Of the thirty locomotives supplied by the Swedish firm of A.S.E.A. in 1965 one was equipped, for trial purposes, with thyristor control. This latter is a system that has found great favour on the heavily graded routes in Scandinavia. It is interesting to find that whereas this very powerful Rumanian locomotive has a total weight of 120 tonnes, it can be ballasted to increase the weight, and thus improve the adhesion, to 126 tonnes if necessary. This is a provision for bad weather conditions. The design has become a standard unit in Rumania, where nearly 100 of these locomotives are now in service. Arrangements have been made for them to be manufactured under licence, in Rumania itself, both for domestic use and for export. At a horsepower rating of 7,350, and a maximum starting tractive effort of 42 tonnes, the design can be regarded as one of the most powerful mixed-traffic locomotives in Europe.

93. **Southern Railway, U.S.A.:** triple-deck 'auto rack' cars.

The above is the railway company's official title for this huge vehicle, but it must be remembered that in North America a 'car' is not something to be driven on the highway; it is almost anything that cannot propel itself on the railway, and range from 'gondola' cars for carrying coal to the most luxurious passenger vehicles. The 'auto rack' car of the Southern has been specially designed to transport new automobiles, and each of its three decks can accommodate twelve normal sized North American cars, or fifteen compact ones, such as a British 'mini'. Adjustable ramps at loading and unloading points allow the cars to be driven on or off at any of the three levels. When the practice began of building special car-carriers the sides of the vehicles were left open, so that the contents could be seen. Very often they presented a highly picturesque sight, with numerous cars in different colours. But with increasing experience in the conveyance of cars it has been found desirable to provide some form of protection against the risk of damage, and the white shields running the full length of the vehicle do this. It will be seen however that there is no top protection for the cars on the top deck.

94. **Southern Pacific:** 'Vert-A-Pack' car-carrier.

Under reference 40, mention was made of some of the special vehicles developed for individual traders on the nominated freight trains of British Railways. The present illustration shows a remarkable American example of a 'car' designed not as a general automobile carrier, but specially for delivery from plant of one particular make, the Chevrolet 'Vega'. This remarkable vehicle was a joint conception of the Southern Pacific Railroad, and General Motors, and as the name 'Vert-A-Pac' suggests the automobiles are loaded in a vertical position. Once inside they are completely enclosed, and as the statements by both railway company and General Motors significantly explain, they are protected from the weather, pilferage and vandalism. One of these fine vehicles carries a total of thirty Vegas.

95. **Denver & Rio Grande Western:** 86 ft (*25 m*) high cube box-car.

The 'Rio Grande', both in name and history is one of the most romantic of American railroads. The imagination is stirred by stories of the pioneer narrow gauge trains nosing their ways into the tremendous canyons of the Colorado Rockies, and in later

years, on the standard gauge some of the later steam locomotives were the size and equal in power and efficiency of almost any in the American continent. Now, when the Rio Grande has entered into its second century of operation it has, both in motive power and rolling stock, units fitting to its proud history. The vehicle illustrated may be nothing more than a box-car; but what a box-car! It is 86 ft (*25 m*) long, and built up to the maximum height of the loading gauge, and, of course, runs on roller bearings. It is in such modern vehicles that the freight goes through the heart of the Colorado Rockies from Denver to Salt Lake City.

96. **Louisville & Nashville:** the 'Stackback' flat car.

The illustrations in this group show various modern methods of carrying automobiles on the railways; and in this connection it may be added that the Rio Grande uses for this purpose triple-deck cars of a similar type to those of the Southern. But in this Louisville and Nashville example it is a case of transporting heavy lorries, or 'trucks' as they are known in North America. As in Europe these are delivered from the builders with nothing more than the chassis and the driver's cab allowing the eventual owner to have a body fitted to suit his particular business. In providing railway transport for deliveries of the chassis the Louisville and Nashville has devised the ingenious method of stacking the maximum number into the minimum of space. In this instance there is no question of having two, still less three tiers; but the inclined arrangement certainly provides a very neat solution. The basic railway vehicle on which they are conveyed is a special and very long form of flat car. It would seem that so far it has not been found necessary to provide any side protection for these massive lorries.

97. Austrian Federal Railways: the 'Transalpin' fast multiple-unit train.

This fast service, which is operated jointly by the Swiss and Austrian railways, runs between Basle and Vienna, via the Arlberg route. The handsome six-car train consists of a driving unit, three trailer cars, a restaurant car, and a driving trailer. The trailer, which is at the opposite end of the train to the driving unit, includes a passenger compartment and a driver's cab to permit direction-reversing in dead end stations with changing the driving unit. The train has seating for 66 first-class passengers and 171 second-class. It is entirely a daytime run, in both directions covering the 585 miles (940 km) in 10½ hours. The principal stations served are Zürich, Sargans Buchs, Innsbruck, Salzburg and Linz. Much of the journey is highly picturesque and the comfort of the seating and the spacious windows make the ride doubly enjoyable. The maximum permitted speed of the train is 93 m.p.h. (150 km/h), and this is attained on the less mountainous part of the route, east of Salzburg.

98. British Railways: the 'H.S.T.'

The High Speed Train, diesel powered, with which some very fast experimental runs were made in 1973, has been designed and developed to take over the major inter-city services on non-electrified lines in Great Britain. It has been designed for a maximum operating speed of 125 m.p.h. (200 km/h). It is the British equivalent of the European 'T.E.E.' trains, though required to work over a railway network that is, in general, much more heavily used. The prototype train was formed of seven air-conditioned passenger coaches of a new design, 75 ft long (22 m) and incorporating the Mark III details of suspension. Because of their much increased length the coaches provide greater seating capacity than the present locomotive-hauled stock, and in greater passenger comfort has accommodation for 96 first-class, and 276 second-class passengers. The power cars, each of 2,250 horsepower are quite separate from the passenger vehicles, and are at each end of the train, making nine vehicles in all. During the trial runs in June 1973 a maximum speed of 143 m.p.h. (230 km/h) was attained between Darlington and York, and on a later run in August 1973 when I was one of the privileged guests of British Railways I logged one half-mile at 138½ m.p.h. (222 km/h) near Thirsk.

99. Netherlands Railways: high-speed inter-city electric train.

The modern railway network of Holland is served entirely, so far as passenger business is concerned, by an intricate system of fast multiple-unit trains. The majority of these are electric, but in the less densely populated parts of the country, north-east of the Zuider Zee the lines are not yet electrified and diesel rail-car sets are used. The pattern of train service is built up on a number of fast, relatively local services, connecting with each other, and involving minimum waiting times for passengers at junctions when change of train has to be made. Great importance is placed both on speed and punctuality, and some remarkable developments in methods of train regulation, by computer, are being introduced on a wide scale. Our picture shows a two-car set; but these can be coupled in multiple to make much longer trains when necessary. Travelling in Holland today one sees the multiple-unit trains in different colours; but the bright yellow in our picture is the new standard, with the bright blue diagonal stripes to indicate the whereabouts of the first-class accommodation. The maximum service speed of these trains is 87 m.p.h. (*140 km/h*).

100. The Diesel 'T.E.E.' Express Train, 'Parsifal'.

The 'Parsifal' is one of the international T.E.E. trains, operated jointly by the S.N.C.F. and the West German Federal Railways. It runs between Paris and Hamburg, serving a remarkable succession of highly industrial regions: Charleroi, Liege, Aachen, Cologne, Dusseldorf, Essen,

Osnabruck and Bremen – to mention only a few of the large centres served. The end-to-end time from Paris to Hamburg is a little over 9 hours. When the train was inaugurated, French motive power and rolling stock was used; but from May 1960 until the winter of 1968 this was replaced by German equipment, as shown in our picture. The train is composed of a power unit at each end, and of the five trailer cars one is a restaurant with kitchen, one a restaurant with bar. Of the three coaches one is an 'open' saloon with centre gangway, while the other two are of the compartment type. These three coaches provide seating for 105 passengers (first-class only) while there are another 46 seats in the two restaurant cars. It is in every way a luxury train.

101. S.N.C.F.: the 'CC-6500' class 1,500-volt high-speed locomotive.

Although the 25,000 volt a.c. system of electrification, at 50 cycles per second, has now been standardised in France, some of the routes over which the fastest daily running is at present performed are equipped with the older system of 1,500 volts d.c. These are the Bordeaux and Toulouse main lines of the former P.O.– Midi system, and the P.L.M., between Paris and Marseilles. Over the Bordeaux and Toulouse routes there are operated trains that run at 125 m.p.h. (*200 km/h*) in daily service. These are not lightweight formations, but assemblages of the massive 'Grand Confort' air conditioned stock and frequently make up a gross trailing load of more than 600 tons. Because the speed of 125 m.p.h. (*200 km/h*) has to be maintained regardless of gradient on those sections of line that are suitable for such speeds a locomotive of exceptional power is needed, and the striking machine illustrated is one of a class capable of an output of about 8,000 horsepower. On the line to Marseilles these locomotives take trains of 700 tons up a gradient of 1 in 125 at 95 m.p.h. (*153 km/h*).

102. **German Federal Railways:** the '103' class, high-speed electric locomotive.

Under references 70 and 71 the beautiful coaching stock used on the 'Rheingold' express was described. Our present picture shows the type of locomotive used for hauling the train. This is required to run at 100 m.p.h. (*160 km/h*) on certain sections of the route, and very great care is taken to provide the drivers with the fullest information to ensure punctual operation. In the cab there is a 'handbook', landscape shaped, which provides a chart of the entire route showing position of stations, changes of gradient, the maximum speeds that may be run over each section, and the speed that is necessary to maintain schedule time of the train itself. As the journey proceeds the pages are turned over, so as to keep the current position constantly in front of the driver. The differences between the maximum speed allowed and the scheduled speed of the train is a measure of the

amount of the so-called 'recovery time' that is available to the driver when running late; though this is apt to be more a theoretical than a practical quantity. It is only the locomotives set aside for working the T.E.E. trains that are painted in the red and cream livery.

103. **British Railways:** the class '87' electric locomotive.

When the main line of the London Midland Region was electrified between London, Liverpool and Manchester, and electric locomotives by a number of different manufacturers were introduced, it was intended that the entire stud should be 'common-user'; in other words any locomotive could be put on to any job, passenger or goods alike. But in the eight years since the introduction of the full service in 1966 much experience has been gained with the different varieties of locomotive – all of which nevertheless look very much alike! – and when the time came to extend the electrification to Glasgow, and new locomotives were needed, it was felt desirable to introduce various modifications in design, particularly to improve the riding qualities. The class '87' was the result, and these have proved remarkably successful machines, not only having improved tractive ability, but riding incomparably more smoothly. These locomotives are now used on the 'Electric Scots' the fastest of which average 80 m.p.h. (*128 km/h*) throughout over the 401½ miles between London and Glasgow. The schedules demand the maintenance of speeds of more than 80 m.p.h. (*128 km/h*) up long gradients of 1 in 75 in the north country, with train loads of about 430 tons.

104. Jugoslav Railways: Swedish-built type 'J2-441' electric locomotive.

This fine example of a 25,000 volt, 50 cycles, locomotive is based on the A.S.E.A. (Swedish) 'Rb 1' model, after this increasingly popular system of traction was chosen for the electrification of the Jugoslav Railways. A decision was made to have locomotives of universal application for passenger and freight alike, and since the A.S.E.A. 'Rb 1', of 5,550 horsepower was ideal for this assignment, orders were placed for 195 units. The majority of the electrical parts were manufactured in Sweden, while the mechanical parts, and the assembly of the complete locomotives were undertaken by the Simmering-Graz-Pauker Company of Graz, Austria, not very far from the Jugoslav frontier. There the new locomotives went by the name of 'Jugo-Loks'. In size and weight they are very similar to the British class '87' having a total weight of 80 tons, but the maximum service speed is only 75 m.p.h. (*120 km/h*). Some of these locomotives are fitted with dynamic braking which is particularly suitable for service on steep mountain gradients such as are encountered on many sections of the Jugoslav railways. The type has proved so successful that it is now being made, under licence, in Jugoslavia, both for the home and export markets.

105. Pakistan Western Railway: British-built electric main line locomotive.

This railway, with its headquarters at Lahore, comprises practically the whole of the former North-Western Railway of British India, except for the lines running south-eastwards to Delhi, in the Punjab, which are now in the Republic of India. It is a large railway with a great variety of operating conditions ranging from the intense traffic in the valley of the Indus to the remote and difficult sections in the mountains of the North-West Frontier. Electrification is now in progress on the busiest lines radiating from Lahore, on the line running north to Rawalpindi, and on the western line to Khanewal. Both these projects involve route mileages of around 200 (*320 km*), and form the first sections of conversion of the two great main lines of the country, to Peshawar, in the frontier regions, and down the Indus valley to Karachi, a long line that is already double tracked throughout its length of nearly 600 miles (*960 km*). The system of electrification is the same as that of the later installations in India, namely 25,000 volts a.c. at 50 cycles per second.

106. Malayan Railways: the '22' class Co+Co main line diesel-electric locomotive.

The Malayan Railways were among the earlier administrations in Asia to introduce diesel-electric traction, though at first it was done on no more than a limited scale and was primarily for operating the long-distance passenger and mail trains. After very careful preparation of the maintenance facilities in the works at Sentul, near Kuala Lumpur, with complete separation of the steam from the incoming diesel activity, a batch of 1,500 horsepower locomotives of the 'first generation' English Electric nose-cab type was introduced with remarkable success. In the meantime most of the freight continued to be worked by steam. In recent years however a batch of forty diesels of an enlarged design has been supplied from Great Britain by B.R.E.-Metro Ltd. These are of the Co+Co type, with an engine horse-power of 1,750, as shown in our picture. At the time when the first Malayan diesels were introduced a livery of leaf green was adopted, and the locomotives were named after flowers of the Malayan countryside. The new locomotives are finished in the new standard livery and carry the full title of the railway on their flanks.

107. **South-Eastern Railway of India:** main line electric locomotive 'WAG3' class.

The present South-Eastern Railway includes the entire network of the former Bengal Nagpur Railway, one of the last of the railways of the former Indian Empire to remain under private company management. The company was formed in 1887 and was taken over by the Government in October 1944. As the Bengal Nagpur Railway it worked in co-operation with the Great Indian Peninsula Railway in operating the Bombay–Calcutta mail service, and had a notable stud of powerful steam locomotives. While serving some of the largest coal areas of India the mineral traffic was also heavy, and a large proportion of its lines are now electrified on the 25,000 volt a.c. system. Some fine electric locomotives were supplied to India by the 50 c/s Group, of the Bo+Bo type with control equipment of the latest type; and in furtherance of general policy, the construction of further locomotives of the same type is being transferred, stage by stage, to local industry in India, under licensing arrangements. The first stage was the building of the mechanical parts, with electrical equipment still being supplied from Europe; but still later manufacture of the electrical parts has also been done in India. By now, nearly 400 of these locomotives are working in India.

108. **Hungarian State Railways:** Bo+Bo general purpose electric locomotive.

Hungary was early in the field of railway electrification in Europe, and in 1935 the line from Budapest to Hegyeshalom was equipped on the 50 cycles per second system, but at a pressure of no more than 16,000 volts instead of the 25,000 volts now favoured. Of course the capital city of Budapest had for many years before this been in the forefront of railway electric traction equipment through the activities of the famous firm of Ganz & Co. In the year after World War II however the French development of electrification at 25,000 volts a.c. to use a colloquialism, had fairly 'started something', and by the year 1960 the Hungarian State Railways had decided to adopt it for all future work and to convert the older lines as and when possible. The first 25,000 volt locomotives were ordered in 1960, and with these proving very successful licensing arrangements were made with the 50 c/s Group for the manufacture of the main electrical and mechanical parts in Hungary. Since then, nearly 200 of the type have been put into traffic.

109–110. **Spanish Frontier Gauge Changing.**

As long ago as 1844 the track gauge of the Spanish railways was laid down as 6 Castillian feet – 5 ft 5½ in. (*1·65 m*) in British Imperial measure. At that time the idea that one day the railways of Spain might be linked with those of the rest of Europe does not seem to have occurred to anyone, in the Peninsula anyway. But the railway link between Spain and France was made no more than twenty years later, and from then, for more than one hundred years, passengers had to change trains at the frontier points. By then however a Spanish engineer had found the solution, from what is known as the Talgo technique. The Talgo trains, which had been running on Spanish railways for nearly twenty years had the coach wheels mounted independently instead of both on a common

axle, and it was this technique that gave rise to the idea that the distance between the wheels could be changed to suit the gauge. To understand how this could be done one has got to study the drawings under references 109 and 110 simultaneously. The picture reference 109 shows the actual installation with a train approaching, while 110 shows what happens when it enters the 'house' at dead slow speed. It must be appreciated at the start that the Talgo train has no axles, as such; the wheels are mounted in a specially shaped steel casting, coloured in grey.

Assume that the train is entering from the top of the page (ref. 110) on Spanish track. The first thing that happens is that the outer flanges of the wheel support casting slide on to the outer supports, of which the top surfaces are shown coloured blue. A very slight lifting action takes the weight off the wheels, and then they pass on to the section where there are no rails at all. Then the unlocking ramps are approached. The tops of these, which are coloured red are of T-section, then engage in the slots of the locking tappets on the wheel support castings, also shown in red. The shape of the ramp draws the locking tappet down, and when it is fully withdrawn, the wheel itself is free to slide sideways. It is guided across from the Spanish to the 'International gauge' by the rails coloured green, and when in the new position the red ramps press the locking tappets upward again, locking the wheels in their new position. They are then ready to make contact with the rails at 4 ft 8½ in. (*1·4 m*) and with the outer edges of the support casting passing clear of the 'blue' rails, normal running is resumed.

111–112. New European High-Speed Networks.

In France the S.N.C.F. has estimated that the main line of the former P.L.M. between Paris and Dijon will be saturated by the year 1980. It includes a number of double track sections, particularly on the steeply graded stretch through the Côte d'Or mountains, and the bold decision has been taken to construct an entirely new line from Combs la Ville to Lyons on which continuous running at 162 m.p.h. (*260 km/h*) will be made, and which will be capable of handling speeds up to 185 m.p.h. (*300 km/h*) in future. At the present time the fastest train between Paris and Lyons, 317½ miles (*615 km*), is 3 hr 44 min. On the new line, with sustained speeds of 160 m.p.h. (*260 km/h*) the time will be cut to exactly 2 hr. This shows an average of about 150 m.p.h. (*220 km/h*). The mileage by the new line will be considerably shorter. The pictorial map shows the present and new routes. Although the latter is primarily for traffic to Lyons and points south, there will be connecting links to enable trains for Dijon and Switzerland via Vallorbe to take advantage of it up to Aisy, while at Macon there will be connection with the line to Italy via the Mont Cenis tunnel. Divergence from the present main line begins at Combs la Ville, 16 miles (*25 km*) out of Paris, and it links up with the existing network at

Sathonay. The gradients through the Côte d'Or mountains, west of Dijon, will be severe; but this is considered no handicap to the very powerful locomotives that will be used.

In West Germany, as the pictorial drawing shows, a most comprehensive new high-speed network is planned, in three successive stages, and work has already started on the first section from Hanover to Gemunden. This will eventually provide an entirely new railway system linking up all the major cities in West Germany. All these new lines are designed for a maximum speed of 185 m.p.h. (*300 km/h*). While the projected new French line from Paris to Lyons is intended purely for passenger traffic, the German high-speed routes will be used for freight trains during the night. There is an important difference in the two cases. The German routes are mainly concerned with internal traffic, whereas the Paris–Lyons route carries a very heavy night passenger train service to the Mediterranean coast as well as to Italy and Switzerland. At holiday times, and in the summer and winter tourist seasons, the former P.L.M. line is busier at night than during the day so that one can understand the intention to use the new route purely for passenger trains.

113. Great Western Railway (England): the preserved 4–6–0 locomotive *Burton Agnes Hall*

The Great Western 'Hall' class was one of the most popular and successful among British medium-power mixed traffic designs. It was in the first place an adaptation of Churchward's famous 2-cylinder express passenger 4–6–0 of the 'Saint' class, which in its original non-superheated form dated from 1903. It was in 1925 that the express engine No. 2925 *Saint Martin* was rebuilt with 6 ft 0 in. (*1·8 m*) coupled wheels instead of the original 6 ft 8½ in. (*2 m*). For three years this engine ran as an isolated prototype. Then in 1928 production of the 'Hall' class proper began. By the year 1944 a total of no less than 258 were in service. Then came the Hawksworth modified design, with redesigned boiler, 'one piece' main frame and plate frame bogie. Another seventy-one engines of this later variety were built, and the engine that has been preserved under the auspices of the Great Western Society, No. 6998 *Burton Agnes Hall* is one of this category. By this time the class was so numerous there had become an acute shortage of names of country houses in Great Western territory and some took their titles from famous homes far afield, in the Lake District, and in Yorkshire. Burton Agnes is on the former North-Eastern line to Bridlington about 5 miles (*8 km*) south-west of that breezy east coast resort.

114. **Canadian National Railways:** the preserved 'U–1–f' 4–8–2 locomotive No. 6060.

This great locomotive was built in 1944 by the Montreal Locomotive Works in response to the need for more heavy main line power in the latter stages of World War II. The engines of her class worked between Montreal and Halifax (Nova Scotia) and between Toronto and Sarnia, but the days of the diesels were coming. She was removed out to Manitoba, and in 1962 after a relatively short life of eighteen years was withdrawn, but placed on exhibition at Jasper station in the Rockies. There No. 6060 remained, kept in spanking external condition, through the loving care of a few local railwaymen. Then in 1971 a replacement was needed for the great 4–8–4 No. 6218 hitherto used on special excursion trains, and the choice fell upon 6060. A 'U–1–a' class No. 6015 was available to replace her as an exhibition engine at Jasper, and No. 6060 was brought to Pointe St. Charles shops, Montreal, for complete overhaul. It was a long job, but by September 1973 it was finished, and the big engine, in pristine condition, was displayed to an enthusiastic public. From that time onwards she has fulfilled her role as a hauler of special trains and today no more popular locomotive runs the rails in Canada.

115. **South Australian Railways:** the preserved lightweight 4–8–4 *Sir Malcolm Barclay-Harvey.*

This locomotive, which though looking so large and impressive, is actually a lightweight, is an exact contemporary of the Canadian National No. 6060, both having been built in 1944. But the South Australia '520' class although running on the 5 ft 3 in. (*1·6 m*) gauge was designed for those sections of the line laid with rails only 60 lb (27 kg) to the yard (0·9 m). The maximum axle load is only 15 tons, and the whole engine weighs only 104 tons. By contrast No. 6060 turns the scale at 150 tons. The South Australian '520' class was artistically styled, with the front very similar to that of the giant Pennsylvania 4–4–4–4s of the '6110' class. When the question arose of maintaining steam locomotives in South Australia for the many enthusiasts, the '520' class 4–8–4 seemed an ideal unit, because due to its light axle-loading it could travel on the 5 ft 3 in. (1·6 m) gauge lines anywhere in the State. The pioneer engine of the class was chosen for preservation, as so far as the name is concerned, none could have been more appropriate. Sir Malcolm Barclay-Harvey was not only Governor General of South Australia at the time the locomotives were first introduced, but was a railway enthusiast of the first order, and was the author of a notable book on the Great North of Scotland Railway.

116. **Cape Breton Steam Railway, Nova Scotia:** the English 'Schools' class 4–4–0 *Repton*.

To the collection of locomotives assembled at the Steamtown Railway Museum, Bellows Falls, Vermont, U.S.A., went one of the celebrated 'Schools' class 4–4–0s of the Southern Railway of England, No. 926 *Repton*, a notable runner first on the fast London–Portsmouth expresses, and later doing even finer work on the heavy Waterloo and Bournemouth

trains. In 1974 however *Repton* was leased to the Cape Breton Steam Railway, located in Glace Bay, Nova Scotia, and put into running order for working regular trains during the summer season. To make her suitable for this passenger working she had to have a number of North American fittings added, including a pilot (cowcatcher), Westinghouse brake, headlight and centre couplers. With these additions her appearance was certainly changed; and while an American bell was added the British whistle was retained. Another new feature was a drop grate. She is proving very popular with her new owners, and operated on a twice daily 20 mile (32 km) round trip through the summer. On the Cape Breton Railway she is known affectionately as the 'New Girl', in distinction to an old Schenectady 2–6–0 of 1899, known as the 'Old Girl'.

117. **Turkish Railways:** a Pullman seat passenger train.

There is an old time aura of romance about railways in Istanbul. It was the eastern terminus of the fabulous Orient Express; one crosses the Bosphorus by the Haydarpasa ferry, and from the terminus station on the Asiatic side great named trains start for distant parts – the Anatolian Express, the Taurus Express, and so on. It is a long journey by train from Istanbul to Baghdad, and in past years it could have been something of an endurance test for those who could not afford the luxury of a sleeping car of the 'Wagon-Lit' company. More recently however new carriages of modern design have been introduced on the Turkish railways, and the so-called 'Pullman seat' type provides maximum comfort for those who have to sit up all night. These handsome cars were built in the Turkish Railways' own workshops at Adapazari.

118. **Seaboard Coast Line:** one of the latest dining cars.

The Seaboard Coast Line Railroad Company was formed in 1967 by an amalgamation of the Seaboard Air Line and the Atlantic Coast Line, with main lines running south from Richmond, Virginia, to Florida. But the Atlantic Coast Line had financial connections with the Louisville and Nashville Railroad, and during 1971 the Seaboard Coast Line became owner in excess of 98 per cent of the capital stock of the Louisville and Nashville. Since the amalgamation of 1967 there has been a general re-organisation of the equipment, and our picture shows one of the latest dining cars, which are of similar structure design to the Tavern-Lounge cars run on some of the principal trains. The seating arrangements in the dining cars are unusual by European standards, in that the tables are set diagonal-wise along each side wall, with settee-type seats encompassing them on two sides. Diners therefore sit facing each other across the car with a wide centre gangway between for the stewards. Nearly half the length of these great 85 ft (*35 m*) long cars is given up to the kitchens and

service pantries. The 'saloon' provides seating for no more than 36 patrons.

119. **British Railways:** the Mark III coach for high-speed trains.

Under reference 98 the philosophy and service potentials of the new 'H.S.T.' are described. The coaches themselves are of a completely new design, fully air-conditioned, and equipped with air filtration to keep the interiors clean. Air springs are used for the secondary suspension, and these give a softer ride for the passengers as well as needing less maintenance. Unlike the prestige trains on the continent of Europe the 'H.S.T.' provides accommodation for both first- and second-class passengers. The coach bodies are the same for both classes, but with different seating arrangements; there are spaces in the open saloon coaches for 48 first class, or 72 'seconds'. These coaches are the longest ever built for service in Great Britain, and measure 75 ft 2 in. (*22 m*) overall. In earlier years the Great Western Railway standardised 70 ft (*21 m*) coaches for main line express work, with a few special purpose vehicles a little longer; but it emphasises the increased amenities of accommodation in the 'H.S.T.' to add that the G.W.R. 70 ft (*21 m*) coaches had seating for 80 passengers. Furthermore the seven trailer cars of the 'H.S.T.' weigh only 245 tons tare, or an average of 35 tons each, despite their great length, whereas the G.W.R. 70 ft (*21 m*) stock of 1923 weighed 38 tons.

120. **Spanish National Railways (R.E.N.F.E.):** coach of the Talgo train.

This illustration shows one of the car units of the 'Catalan Talgo', the latest development of the Talgo principles of coach construction, which incorporates the following basic principles: the axles are guided *on* the rail, and not *by* the rail; the wheels are independent as described in the references to the gauge changing equipment (refs. 109, 110); the car bodies are articulated to form a single integrated chain of cars in the train, and they have a very low centre of gravity. The 'Catalan Talgo', which runs between Barcelona and Geneva, has a normal complement of 14 cars: 9 first class, each seating 17 passengers; 2 dining cars; 1 kitchen car, and 2 service cars. This formation is extended on occasions to include 2 additional first-class cars. The individual cars are very short, and the normal train provides seating in the ordinary cars for 153 passengers; in each of the dining-cars there is seating for 24. With the aid of the gauge changing apparatus the train runs through, as a Trans-Europe-Express, over the railways of three countries, Spain, France and Switzerland, the route being via Cerbere, Narbonne, Avignon, Valence, Grenoble, Aix les Bains and Culoz.

121. **South African Railways:** double-tier car-carrier.

The 3 ft 6 in. (*1·2 m*) gauge is no handicap to the introduction of vehicle carriers, though naturally the capacity cannot be made so great as on some of the railways in North America. They carry eight vehicles, four per deck. Each wagon is fitted with bridge plates, which, when lowered allow the vehicles to be driven along the train under their own power during loading and unloading operations. Tie-down winches, four per vehicle, hold them securely during transit. These winches can be adjusted as to position to enable different sizes of vehicles to be accommodated. These fine wagons were ordered in the first place to make up a unit train of fifty, operating as a 'block' between Aloes Siding, Port Elizabeth, and Kaalfontein, near Kempton Park in the Transvaal. This fifty wagon train is two-thirds of a mile long, and makes an impressive sight when fully loaded with 400 cars.

122. **South Africa:** side dump wagon for Iscor.

This remarkable wagon, one of twenty-five built by Dorman Long (Africa) Ltd for Iscor, is primarily a steel-works vehicle, designed for the handling of blast furnace and steel melting plant waste, which is hauled to the top of slag dumps, and disposed of by tipping. The design however comes under the surveillance of the South African Railways, and in basing it upon an American design, some considerable modifications were called for by the railway administration. Dumping to either side is possible by means of wagon-body-tilting on dual side pivots. The tilting operation is manually controlled, though the power is provided by the large compressed air cylinders, seen with their pistons extended in our picture. There are two cylinders on either side, and as will be appreciated these work in pairs. The South African specification called for a much heavier body than that of the American counterpart, with massive reinforcement at the ends to withstand an accidental blow from one of the big swinging grabs by which the wagons are loaded.

123. **New Zealand Railways:** 42-ton bottom discharge coal hopper wagon.

This is another striking example of a large special-purpose vehicle built for use on a railway working on sub-standard gauge. The New Zealand Railways operate on the 3 ft 6 in. (*1·2 m*) gauge, and the fine wagon illustrated has been designed for bulk conveyance of coal from mine to power station. Its overall length is 50 ft 5 in. (*15 m*), and it accommodates a pay-load of 42 tons. The bottom discharge feature enables a train of such wagons to be hauled slowly over an open gallery, discharging the coal, one by one from successive vehicles on to a belt conveyed below.

124. **Victorian Railways:** Bulk grain wagon.

The domestic services of the Australian State of Victoria are operated on the spacious 5 ft 3 in. (*1·6 m*) gauge, and this naturally allows the

running of large, wide vehicles. At the same time Victoria is faced with the inconvenience of other rail gauges in neighbouring States, and on certain through runs special vehicles are used on which the bogies are changed at the point where there is a break of gauge. The vehicles are lifted bodily from one set of bogies and lowered on to a second set, for the altered gauge. At the frontier between New South Wales and Victoria, it is not unusual for about 20,000 vehicles to be bogie-exchanged in a year. No such procedure is necessary with the handsome bulk grain wagons illustrated, which were built specially for internal traffic within the State of Victoria. They have a capacity of 53 tons and were first introduced in 1968. They are painted in a colour symbolical of the golden wheat they were designed to carry.

125–128. **The A.M.T.R.A.K. Evolution.**

The setting up of the National Railroad Passenger corporation has already been noticed in this book under reference 85, and four illustrations show some of the restyled and new equipment, which is certainly making a strong impact, visually at any rate, upon the travelling public of the U.S.A.

125. **A Pennsylvania High-Speed Electric Locomotive, Repainted in the 'A.M.T.R.A.K.' Colours.**

This is one of the best known electric locomotives types in North America, known as the 'GGI' class. They operate on 11,000 volts a.c. at 25 cycles per second, and have the wheel arrangement 2–Co–Co–2. They would nowadays however be considered very heavy locomotives for the power developed, because for a horsepower of 4,620 their weight is 205 tons. By comparison the latest British locomotive of class '87' develop considerably more than 4,620 h.p. and yet weigh no more than 80 tons. The 'GGI' have a fine record of fast, reliable service on the New York–Washington run on which the maximum speed is 100 m.p.h. (*160 km/h*). These famous locomotives certainly look very gay in the new A.M.T.R.A.K. colours.

126. The French-built Turbo Train.

Ever since the introduction of the gas turbine as a prime mover in aircraft design – the now familiar 'jet' engine – designers have sought to incorporate the principle into railway traction. There have been gas turbine locomotives in Switzerland, Great Britain and the U.S.A. that have met with varying degrees of success; but one of the few to develop into a real 'bread and butter' dividend-earning proposition is that used in France, on the Paris–Cherbourg line of the S.N.C.F. and first introduced in 1970. This used an 820 kw aero-gas turbine set with hydraulic transmission, and ran up to speeds of 125 m.p.h. (*200 km/h*). It is a train of similar type that has

been purchased by A.M.T.R.A.K. and is here illustrated. In the meantime the French are developing the still more revolutionary T.G.V. trains of which the first experimental unit is described under reference 2 in this book.

127. The strikingly-styled 'Metroliner'.

The express service over the former Pennsylvania route between New York and Washington is now being operated by the new Budd cars illustrated. They are capable of speeds up to 160 m.p.h. (*256 km/h*), though actually they do not need to run at more than 125 m.p.h. (*200 km/h*). To this speed they can accelerate from rest in less than 2 minutes. The fastest run over the 227 miles between New York and Washington was 3 hr. 35 min., an average of 63·5 m.p.h. (*100 km/h*); with the new cars the time is expected to be 2 hr. 55 min. at 77·5 m.p.h. (*125 km/h*). The cars are very large, 85 ft. (*136 m*) long over couplers, and weigh around 75 tons. Each one is a separately contained power unit, with driver's cab at one end, and having all axles powered. Each car has four motors, with a total horsepower of 2,560, at 100 m.p.h. (*160 km/h*). This, of course, provides a tremendous capacity for acceleration. The cars can be coupled in multiple, for operation by a single driver, in any number up to twenty cars. There are two classes of passenger provided for: 'coach', with seating for 76 in a car, or 'parlor car' with seating for 34. There are also what are termed 'snack coaches', with seating for 60 passengers. These trains are essentially short-distance inter-city units, on which an elaborate full meal service is not called for.

128. **What the new super-power will look like.**

For the train services of the future A.M.T.R.A.K. is purchasing the General Electric Company's recently developed new range of very powerful electric locomotives known as the Model 'E 60 C', developing 6,000 horsepower, and it is interesting to compare the general style and physical characteristics of these locomotives with those of the Pennsylvania 'GG1' class (ref. 125). First of all there is the wheel arrangement. When electric locomotives were built for high-speed passenger service it was thought essential to have a two-wheeled truck, or leading bogie in front of the powered wheels, and the 'GG1' had four-wheeled bogies fore and aft. The French exploded that theory with their 1,500 volt locomotives of the 'CC-7100' and 'BB-9200' classes, and the new A.M.T.R.A.K. power is of the Co–Co type – all adhesion. The casing has now become almost completely air-smoothed, if not exactly streamlined, and the weight, for a 6,000 horsepower locomotive is 190 tons, as compared with 205 tons for 4,620 horsepower in the Pennsylvania case. These locomotives operate on the 11,000 volt, 25 cycles per second a.c. system.

129. **Automatic Car Identification:** a colour coded panel as seen on a Santa Fé car.

In North America, although there have been a number of amalgamations lately reducing the number of individual railway companies and setting up big combines like Penn-Central, the Burlington Northern and so on, there are still a vast number of different owners and an equally great variety of cars. With the approach to computerising the operational controls in great marshalling yards some mechanised process was necessary to eliminate the human recording of wagon types, ownership and destination of individual loads as freight trains came into the reception sidings at marshalling yards. In former days an operator walked the length of the train noting all the necessary information on what was called a 'cut-card'. This was sent by pneumatic tube to the control room of the yard, so that when shunting began and wagons began to run down the hump the operator in the control room could switch wagons into their correct classification sidings. But in modern practice that operation can be done by computer, and the computer required to know destinations, weights, and such like, so that it could apply the appropriate controls. The Association of American Railroads (A.A.R.) of which the various Canadian railways are also members, have adopted the principle of Automatic Car Identification, and a colour-coded panel is now affixed to every freight vehicle in major railway service. The panel is a rectangle 24 in. ($o \cdot 6$ m) high and 10 in. ($o \cdot 2$ m) wide, and includes fourteen horizontal strips of colour, combinations of red, blue, black and white. By varying the relation of the adjacent colours one with another, a very large number of codes are obtained, which when decoded can identify the type of vehicle and the owning railway.

130. **Automatic Car Identification:** the detecting apparatus directed towards a Penn-Central car.

Having provided the identification codes on the vehicles the next stage is to record the information and transmit it to the control centres where it will be used. At 'key' points along the various lines, such as the entry to major yards, large junctions and such like, there are photo-electric 'scanners' which read the labels as the wagons pass, de-code what they have read by virtually instantaneous electronic methods, and then transmit the information to a computer. The computer then processes the information ready for when it is needed for feeding into other computers concerned with train marshalling, and for keeping an exact check upon where every wagon is. The information is not solely concerned with train movements. The presence of wagons from railways other than the owning company is recorded for subsequent accounting, and the allocation of costs for mileage charges and so on. The process of Automatic Car Identification is just one link in a

magnificent tool of modern automated railway management.

131. **Automatic Train Reporting by Computer.**

On British Railways a novel instant-information service to the various divisional control centres has been devised, making use of modern electronic and computerised techniques. For many years prior to the nationalisation of British Railways the former L.M.S. provided for the routine reporting of train movements at a number of selected timing points along the line. They were originally made by telephone, and later by teleprinter. This process, satisfactory as it proved over the years, necessarily involved a certain time-lag, as well as the operators' time in sending and recording the messages. Today however with the greatly increased speed of traffic, that time-lag could become intolerable and so, linking it in with the train description apparatus in the few major signal boxes a process is activated by the train description in which the time at which trains enter the 'berth' track circuit of every signal is transmitted, instantaneously. A tape record is produced of all train movements in the area, giving up to the minute information of the time of transmission, the signal number from which it was made and the timetable reporting number of the train. This tape record is produced in the divisional control centre at Crewe. When all is flowing smoothly such a record is a matter of routine but one can readily imagine how valuable it is to the divisional controller in the event of some unusual occurrence on the line.

132. New South Wales Government Railways: double-deck power car for Sydney suburban service.

The problem of commuter traffic is world wide. For brief peaks morning and evening railways in the environs of large cities have to provide accommodation for a positive flood of humanity, and in trying to solve the age-old conundrum of how to get a quart into a pint pot recourse has been made on a number of railways to double-deck coaches. One of the difficulties with these was that of getting the large number of passengers for whom accommodation was provided in and out of the doors in the brief periods of a station stop. It was this trouble that made the experiment on the Southern Railway of England unsuccessful. On railways where the service intensity is not so great double-deck cars have been introduced with success. In certain cases the cars were drawn by locomotives, and the N.S.W.G.R. car illustrated is notable as being the first in the world of its kind, and the pioneer of a series of complete eight-car doubledeck trains.

133. Rumanian State Railways: double-decker train.

A very interesting example of this new trend in rolling stock for commuter traffic is provided by some very handsome trains built in East Germany for the Rumanian State Railways. Viewing these impressive cars from outside one might wonder what they were like on the upper deck with the windows apparently small, part vertical, and part sloping in the roof; but a surprising degree of light and airiness has been contrived, through a gay colour scheme of orange walls and light red colouring of the seats. The head rests of the seats are grey and on a level with the change in angle of the windows. These cars certainly represent a most successful example of modern railway carriage design for commuter traffic.

134. New South Wales Government Railways: double-decker train for inter-urban service.

Around Sydney, in addition to its teeming suburbs there are many favoured residential districts lying up to 50 miles distant, and for these the N.S.W.G.R. has introduced some very lavish air-conditioned cars. These operate on the north main line to the furthest extent of the electrification, to Gosford, and the journey on the upper deck of these trains is a delightful experience, climbing through the northern suburbs of Sydney, and then descending steeply in magnificently wooded country to the crossing of the Hawkesbury River. The subsequent run alongside arms of this great estuary is one of the most beautiful in the whole of Australia. The cars can travel fast, though in this very hilly country there is little opportunity for sustained speeding.

135. **CP Rail:** double-deck cars for the Montreal suburban service.

CP Rail, as the successor in name to the Canadian Pacific Railway is fortunate in having the advantage of a loading gauge very much higher than anything in Europe, and the double-deck principle has been applied with great effect on its latest suburban cars. Unlike the Australian and Rumanian examples previously described, these great Canadian cars are hauled by an ordinary locomotive, and a number of the familiar 'first-generation' diesel-electrics from General Motors have been adapted for the purpose. Our picture shows one of the trailer cars marshalled in the middle of a suburban train, but a number have been built as 'driving trailers'. The trains are worked on the 'push-and-pull' principle. The locomotive remains attached at one end, and for the reverse direction of running the engineer rides in the cab of the driving trailer operating the locomotive by remote control. The engineer is on the lower deck, and on the upper deck are much sought after seats looking ahead down the line.

136. **Union Pacific Railroad:** maximum power diesel-electric locomotive.

In the year 1969, the largest single unit diesel-electric locomotive ever produced was put into service on the Union Pacific Railroad. It was called the 'Centennial', by way of commemorating the hundredth anniversary of the driving of the last spike on the first transcontinental route across the U.S.A. It was a 'doubling up' of two of the standard General Motors 3,000 horsepower type on a chassis carried by two eight-wheeled trucks – a type Do–Do locomotive of 6,000 horsepower. This giant unit did not go into quantity production at the La Grange plant because the railways preferred to have smaller units, generally not over 4,000 horsepower that they could couple in multiple. Diesel locomotives to work at maximum efficiency must be going 'all-out'; and with a locomotive so large as the 'Centennial' this would not always be possible. Nevertheless it is a striking example of what can be done.

137. **Western Australian Government Railways:** 2,000 horsepower diesel-electric locomotive for 3 ft 6 in. ($1 \cdot 2$ m) gauge lines.

In recent years the railways of Western Australia have 'hit the headlines', as the saying goes, with the construction of the new standard gauge line from Kalgoorlie to Perth and Fremantle, running iron-ore trains with a payload of 9,000 tons, and the 'Indian Pacific' passenger service between Perth and Sydney. At the same time however there has been notable development on its own domestic 3 ft 6 in. ($1 \cdot 2$ m) gauge system, with heavy tonnages of timber, bauxite, and the coal mined in the south-western corner of the State. For working all kinds of traffic on the 3 ft 6 in. ($1 \cdot 2$ m) gauge lines some fine new 2,000 horsepower diesel-electric locomotives have recently been supplied by

G.E.C. Traction Ltd. These are of the Co–Co type, and have taken over duties previously worked by the powerful 2–8–2 steam locomotives of Type 'V'. The striking difference between the colour schemes of the standard gauge and 3 ft 6 in. ($1 \cdot 2$ m) diesel-electric locomotives of the W.A.G.R. will be apparent from a comparison of items 82 and 137 in this volume.

138. **Erie–Lackawanna:** G.E.C. model 'U34 CH', diesel-electric locomotive.

This railway combination, which dates from 1960, was an amalgamation of the Delaware, Lackawanna and Western and of the Erie Railroad, made at a time when there was a general recession in American railway business, and the two companies had certain duplicating facilities. The Lackawanna was a relative short though busy route between New York City and Buffalo, and the Erie, while duplicating the Buffalo run also had a main line extending to Chicago, and competing for the through traffic with both the Pennsylvania and the New York Central. In the days of recession the business was not enough to sustain two, let alone three routes, and that of the Erie, in addition to that of the N.Y.C. has now been withdrawn. Since 1968 the Erie–Lackawana, though operating independently, has been owned by the Norfolk and Western Railway. The Erie–Lackawanna has however retained its distinctive livery and style, as exemplified in the fine 3,380 horse-power diesel-electric locomotive shown in our picture.

139. **Auto-Train Corporation:** G.E.C. 4,000 horsepower diesel-electric locomotive for car-carrier trains.

The name A.M.T.R.A.K. is associated with the operation of a new, highly rationalised network of passenger services in the U.S.A.; but the new railway set-up in U.S.A. also has diversifications, of which the large diesel-electric locomotive illustrated shows one. In Great Britain the name 'auto-train' signified a small branch set of two or three coaches hauled or propelled by a permanently coupled small tank engine having controls so arranged that the locomotive could be remotely driven from the opposite end of the train. This is seen in the CP Rail double-decker trains (ref. 135). But in the new set-up an 'Auto-train' is a train carrying 'autos' – motor cars, in their hundreds, and even on fairly level gradients requiring all the power of a 4,000 horsepower diesel. This very powerful example of the present G.E.C. range is very strikingly finished in red, white and blue colours though in quite a different style from that of the A.M.T.R.A.K. passenger locomotives illustrated under references 85, 125 and 128 in this volume.

140. **West German Federal Railways:** diagram of the signal control tower at Frankfurt.

This is one of the largest concentrations of signalling control on the continent of Europe, and regulates traffic on all the approach lines, and in the station itself. The philosophy of control is divided into three sections, which can be appreciated, from the plan diagram of the control room. This is contained in the topmost floor of the tower, as shown by the outjutting windows (ref. 142). The nerve centre, in terms of operational control is represented collectively by the positions coloured yellow; by those coloured red, and by those coloured blue. Broadly speaking it can be said that the yellow positions contain the control desks from which the points and signals in the immediate neighbourhood of the station are operated, while the controllers at the red positions exercise general surveillance with particular reference to priorities and the movement of trains from the outer area. The two regulating officials at the blue positions have an overall responsibility for traffic movement in the entire area in and around Frankfurt. In the tower the four floors below the operating room contain the electrical relays and control circuits by which all the interlocking of functions is performed, while the ground floor houses the power generating equipment. In the basement are the batteries.

141. **Frankfurt Signal Box:** inside the control room.

This drawing shows what could be termed the inner sanctum, where the senior regulators work, as shown on the diagram in illustration 140. The

illuminated track diagram in front of them shows an overall picture of train movements. They are not concerned with the details of platform working, shunting, light engine movements in and around the station itself, but rather with the approach and departure of trains to and from the area, and in freight movements avoiding the central passenger station. The reporting numbers of passenger trains are displayed on the diagram as they enter the area, and instructions are sent by push button to the operators at the red positions in the 'open' part of the control room, who in turn supervise the work of the switch panel operators at the yellow positions on illustration 140.

142. **West German Federal Railways (D.B.):** the Frankfurt control tower.

In North America any signal box is called a 'tower', but in Europe the English 'signal box' is simply a 'cabine de manoeuvre' in France, or a 'Stellwerk' in Germany. But the latest installations of highly centralised control, of which Frankfurt is one and Munich is another, are certainly 'towers' in aspect, if not in name; and the great structure at Frankfurt is a tremendous and commanding object standing among the tracks in the very centre of the layout at the platform ends. No traveller can really fail to be aware of it. The Germans call it a 'Gleisbildstellwerk', or a signal box with an illuminated diagram inside. There is great emphasis on the need for the operators to see all the traffic that is flowing, and that is why they are given such an extremely high control room. It will be noticed from both 140, and 142, that the operating floor extends outwards beyond the general line of the building to give a clear view immediately below as well as all around. The difference between this philosophy and that developed in Great Britain, where many large terminal stations are operated from signal cabins when the men do not *see* any trains at all, is striking.

143. **Queensland Government Railways:** the signal box at Rockhampton.

One could detect a strong family likeness between the smart new signal box in Queensland, and the huge one on British Railways (ref. 144). Rockhampton is a relatively small interlocking and formed part of the general modernisation of what was a rather antiquated station layout dating from early colonial days. The Australian conception of a cabin layout, like the British, is to have all the relay and other electrical interlocking and control equipment on the ground floor and only the operating room elevated. At Rockhampton the latter is arranged with a view over the tracks though with a comprehensive illuminated diagram it is not considered necessary to see all that is going on outside. The elaborate sunshade will be noticed. This is not only to afford protection from the *heat* of the sun – and it can

be *very* hot in Rockhampton in the height of the summer! – but to shade the illuminated diagram from strong extraneous light. Otherwise there could be times when the indications on the diagram would be difficult to see.

144. **British Railways:** the signal box at Preston, Lancs.

This huge concentration of control is one of only five signal boxes now regulating traffic between Weaver Junction and Glasgow, a distance of 225 miles (*362 km*). Preston is in some respects the most comprehensive of all, because it controls not only the Anglo-Scottish main line from a point north of Wigan to north of Carnforth, a distance of more than 40 miles (*64 km*) of very heavily worked line, but also a long stretch of cross-country line extending through Blackburn and Burnley to junctions with the Manchester-Leeds main line at Todmorden and Hebden Bridge, Yorkshire. Although there are windows in the control room the signalmen themselves do not see any trains in the course of their day's work on the control panel. They work entirely from the indications displayed on the illuminated track diagram. The extent of the electrical controls will be apparent from the size of the ground floor of the box, which extends beyond the limit of our picture in both directions. Working in conjunction with Preston are no less than eleven unmanned satellite signal boxes, controlled electronically from the Preston panel.

145. Japanese National Railways: pictorial map of nationwide Shin-Kansen network.

The New Tokaido Line between Tokyo and Osaka, providing a 100 m.p.h. (*160 km/h*) service at quarter-hour intervals throughout the day, has been one of the greatest success stories in all railway history, both technically and financially. Today Japan is busily engaged in constructing many extensions. The pictorial map shows the network as now planned, with different colours to indicate the successive stages. The original line has already been extended southwards from Osaka to Okayhama, and several new lines are now being built. When these are completed there will be 1,200 miles (*1,930 km*) in operation, while the map shows that a further 950 miles (*1,530 km*) have been designated for construction as part of the basic plan. It will be seen that these latter include substantial mileages on the islands of Hokkaido in the north, and Kyushu in the south. The former will make use of the undersea tunnel (refs. 86–88). Because of the physical nature of the main Japanese island of Honshu much of the new lines will be within tunnels, burrowing into the central mountain range that forms the backbone of the island. Even this ambitious programme of new railway construction is not enough, and the map shows, in dotted lines, the supplementary network now under active consideration, and which would involve a further 3,400 miles (*5,471 km*) of new high-speed Shin-Kansen lines.

146. Japanese National Railways: a line-up of 'Hikari' lightning trains.

The 'Hikari' or lightning trains, that are putting up such outstanding performances on the sections of the Shin-Kansen network already in operation, are each composed of sixteen cars, streamlined throughout, and with every axle powered. On the original section between Tokyo and Osaka the normal speed is 130 m.p.h. (*210 km/h*), but on the newer sections the maximum will be 160 m.p.h. (*257 km/h*). The speed of these fast trains each carrying on an average 1,000 passengers and running at quarter-hour intervals has necessitated the most elaborate safety precautions. There are no wayside signals, only a speed indicator in the driver's cab telling him the speed at which he may run. These cab signals are controlled by a system of continuous automatic train control with an inductive electrical link between track and train. If a driver should divert from the instructions thus given to him, the brakes would be automatically applied.

147. Japanese National Railways: magnetic levitation research vehicle.

Spectacular as the results have been from the New Tokaido Line, with its 100 m.p.h. (*160 km/h*) service between Tokyo and Osaka, it is now considered that this will not meet the travelling needs of Japan in the foreseeable future. The construction of many extensions will inevitably bring more traffic on to the original section, and instead of duplicating the line thoughts have turned to something infinitely faster still. Research and development work has already started towards the eventual provision of a new line on which the journey time between Tokyo and Osaka will be *one hour* – an average from start to stop of about 280 m.p.h. (*450 km/h*). This is no distant dream of backroom scientists – but an urgent project, because it is thought that the capacity of the existing line will be saturated by 1980. Instead of conventional electric traction the new trains will be propelled by what is known as linear motors, operating by direct electro-magnetic force, and able to develop a maximum speed of more than 300 m.p.h. (*480 km/h*). A test vehicle has already been built and is the subject of much intensive research. The first demonstration of this remarkable looking device was made at the time of the centenary celebrations of the Japanese railways in October 1972, and future progress will be watched with intense interest all over the railway world.

148. **Black Mesa & Lake Powell Railroad:** 50,000 volt, fully automated electric locomotive.

Deep in the heart of America's middle-west near the border of Arizona and Utah and some 130 miles (*21 km*) from the nearest main line railway is the Black Mesa group of open cast coal mines. Astride the State boundary 78 miles (*125 km*) away is the outlet from Lake Powell, where an enormous electricity

generating station has been built; and between the two is the world's latest automated railway. It is a remarkable project in its very isolation. The traffic requirement at the outset was 30,000 tons of coal a day, and studies resulted in a decision to convey this in three loads a day. It was further ascertained that with adequate locomotive power this could be achieved by a single train of eighty-three bottom-dump hopper wagons making three round trips daily each of 156 miles. Diesel traction was ruled out owing to the need to transport fuel, and by using electric traction at the exceptionally high voltage of 50,000 only one sub-station was needed on the whole line. To work this very heavy train three electric locomotives with a continuous horsepower rating of 5,100 have been purchased from G.E.C., each having an output equivalent to a 6,000 horsepower diesel. The train will be driven automatically by coded instructions given by an inductive link up with the track. On the open line an average speed of 35 m.p.h. (*56 km/h*) will be maintained. In its remote, rather romantic situation, in its exceptional electricity supply system for traction, and in the automatic control of its entirely unmanned trains, Black Mesa and Lake Powell is one of the world's most remarkable railways.

149. **Norwegian State Railways:** Co–Co passenger electric locomotive.

It would perhaps be an exaggeration to state that there is not a level mile in the whole of the Norwegian State

Railways' route but in so mountainous a country all lines of railway include some very severe grading. Perhaps the most familiar route to foreign tourists is the main line between Bergen and Oslo which climbs over the rugged mountain chain that runs from north to south throughout the length of Norway. Very powerful electric locomotives are in service and our picture shows one of the latest of the Co–Co type, built in 1968. The small snow ploughs in front of each wheel will be noted. On some of the most vulnerable parts of the line there are lengthy snow sheds and in the depths of winter constant patrolling with powerful rotary ploughs is necessary. The running of trains proceeds summer and winter alike. There is no question of letting bad weather interrupt the service in Norway.

150. Moroccan National Railways: 2,750 kw electric locomotive.

The national railway system in Morocco does not include the entire railway mileage in the country and its two sections are in fact separated by a length of the privately owned Tangiers–Fez Railway. This curious state of affairs is explained by the nationalisation, as from January 1963, of the former Moroccan Railway and the Morocco Eastern Railway which were separated from each other. The former Moroccan Railway has a central stretch along the Atlantic coast between Casablanca and Rabat, with a line running south into the desert country to a terminus at Marrakech, while from Rabat the line turns eastward inland to a junction with the Tangiers–Fez Railway at Sidi Kacem. This line, from Marrakech to Sidi Kacem is electrified throughout on the 3,000 volt d.c. system. In view of the French influence in Morocco this might seem a little strange; but on the other hand the Tangiers–Fez Railway is under joint French and Spanish control, and the modern system of electrification in Spain is 3,000 volts d.c.

151. South Jersey Transit: electric railcar for automatic train operation.

The Delaware River Port Authority owns the celebrated Benjamin Franklin suspension bridge that connects the cities of Philadelphia and Camden across the Delaware River, and in 1936 a 4 mile (6 km) long transit line across the bridge was completed. But this line had become completely outdated, and the new $10\frac{1}{2}$ mile (17 km) South Jersey line has been built on the tracks of the old route, and along the route of the old Pennsylvania–Reading Seashore lines, most of which has now been abandoned to make the new route. The new trains for the South Jersey Transit are designed for automatic operation on the same principles as those of the Victoria Line tube railway in London, except that on the South Jersey line the train attendant has not only to close and *open* the doors, but to push a button to start the automatic train operation. In London the act of closing the doors initiates the starting of the train, and the doors open automatically when the train stops in the next station. The South Jersey transit trains operated on the 600 volt d.c. traction system, with current collection from a third rail.

152. East German State Railways: the Warnemünde train ferry.

From an early date in railway history train ferry services have been operated across the Baltic, and one of the newest and most interesting is that working on the through freight route between Berlin and Copenhagen. The actual ferry is between the East German port of Warnemünde and the Danish port of Gedser, and the ship concerned, the *Warnemünde* is a fine piece of design especially in carrying heavy loads of railway freight. Our picture shows her approaching the loading dock, with the prow lifted to provide the opening for railway vehicles to be propelled on board. The use of this train ferry greatly reduces the distance that would have to be covered in transporting freight from Berlin to Copenhagen if an all-rail route was to be made. Even then one could not avoid some ferry crossings. The rail route from West Germany into Denmark, through the province of Schleswig-Holstein would have to be followed by some 'island hopping' in Denmark itself in order to reach Copenhagen.

ACKNOWLEDGEMENTS

The publishers, author and artists must express their appreciation of the help received from the undermentioned organisations, for photographs details of painting, and of machinery; and no less to the publicity managers of numerous railways throughout the world.

Alsthom; ASEA; Association of American Railroads; BR Engineering; The Budd Co.; CAF; Dorman Long Vanderbijl; Fruehauf Corp.; G.E.C. Traction; General Motors of Canada; Great Western Society; International General Electric Co.; Iron Ore Co. of Canada; Kolmex; Krauss-Maffei; MAN; Maschinen Export; Metro-Camell; MLW Industries; Nohab; Orenstein & Koppel; Rheinstahl Henschel; S.G.P.; S.L.M. Société MTE; Eegmann & Co.: 50 c/s Group.

INDEX